HAVE THE ♀ WOMEN LEFT VENUS?

AF133456

HAVE THE WOMEN LEFT VENUS?
DECODING GENDER @ WORKPLACE

GEET MALA JALOTA

Anecdote
Publishing House
For the love of quality reading!

Anecdote
Publishing House
For the love of quality reading!

anecdotepublishinghouse.com
champreaders.com

Anecdote Publishing House
2nd Floor 2/15 Lane no. 2 Ansari Road,
Daryaganj-110002

Published by Anecdote Publishing House
Copyright © Geet Mala Jalota

First Edition 2024

ISBN 978-81-968952-9-7

MRP ₹ 350

All Rights Reserved.
No part of this publication may be reproduced, stored in a retrieval system, or transmitted in any form, or by any means — electronic, mechanical, photocopying, recording or otherwise — without the prior permission of the publisher. Opinions expressed in it are the author's own. The publisher is in no way responsible for these.

Book Promoted and Marketed by Champ Readers Pvt. Ltd.
Edited by Papri Sen Sri Raman
Cover design by Rishikumar Thakur
Layout by Aaush Kumar
Printed by Thomson Press (India) Ltd, New Delhi

CONTENTS

Reason for Writing This Book — *vii*

Chapter 1 Mirror, Mirror on the Wall — 1

Chapter 2 Rewriting Traditional Roles — 17

Chapter 3 A Woman's World — 35

Chapter 4 Decoding Venus — 49

Chapter 5 A Level playing field — 59

Chapter 6 Strategic implications for women's career — 67

Chapter 7 Discovery — 73
   i. Methodology: — *73*

   ii. Capability Building Interviews — *79*

REASON FOR WRITING THIS BOOK

As a nation, India prides itself on many counts – be it engineering talent, mineral assets, architectural marvels, natural beauty, spiritual heritage, yoga, mathematicians, secularism, world's largest democracy, railway network, religious diversity, traditions and Gandhi.

These metrics are great conversation openers when we talk about India at public and private gatherings. Another achievement of current times which can be added to the list are the strides women are making in breaking down entry barriers in professions like the Army, Aviation, Electric Transmission (Maha Transco), Banking to name a few.

And yet, the ceiling remains. Despite so much being written about financial and nonfinancial benefits of having women as heads of businesses, I still see very few women at department head levels. If educating the girl child was enough guarantee of women reaching the company board positions as CEOs, India would have been among the Top 50 nations of the World Economic Forum (a global thinktank which encourages dialogue and action on regional business issues and therefore shapes regional agendas on health, education, political and employment) rankings.

In reality, India hovers between 123 to 126 among 140 odd countries. That is because, globally, the World Economic Forum (WEF), uses Female Labour Force Participation (FLFP) rate as the key metric to compare the status of women in the work economy, among member countries. This sets standards and benchmarks the effectiveness of women-focused initiatives in health, education, economy and political representation. One parameter is also the difference in average salary of men and women, which is an important indicator of their market value.

About India's performance on this standard, the percentage has been steadily declining since the year 2000, when it was 31%. It plummeted to 21% by 2018 to temporarily rise again in 2019 (24%). Predictably it went down marginally to reach 24% after again in 2022.

According to *The Wire*, '…the LFPR among urban women, women with graduate (or higher) level education, or who were illiterate saw a marginal improvement between 2020-21 and 2021-22. (Figure 2)'

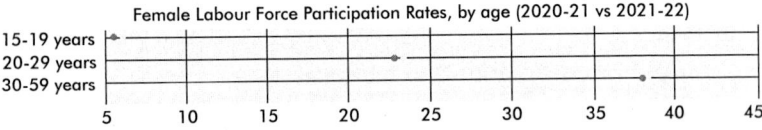
Female Labour Force Participation Rates, by age (2020-21 vs 2021-22)

When I started digging into this metric, as a recruiter, trainer and as a behavioural expert, it was disquieting to note that education was not directly translating into jobs for women in corporate board rooms. Between intention and execution, a link seemed to be missing. That's what I wanted to find out.

So I started putting the available pieces of the puzzle together to find the missing pieces.

As Human Resources (HR) professionals, we have been trained to apply Western models, without understanding the impact of cultural nuances. I hope that my enquiry will bring these out, which will spell out the difference between failure and success of HR initiatives. It was also important to assess how effective are telecommuting, virtual working, flexi-working and part-time jobs, in helping women reach corporate board positions.

What better time to explore this issue, of why women leave the workforce in India and what needs to be done differently, as Diversity and Inclusion becomes Corporate India's next agenda.

CHAPTER 1

MIRROR, MIRROR ON THE WALL

TO GET THE right answer to a question, it is important that the question is clearly spelt out. This is because the quality of the answers will depend on the caliber of questions being asked. When our former Prime Minister, Manmohan Singh (2004-2014) commented that there exists 'a shortage of technical, professional and managerial staff that is constraining growth' he was commenting from the perspective of an economist. An investment in education not bearing fruit is a dead investment. So girls, tell me, are we the dead investments of India?

The Viciousness of the Circle

I met **Priya** when she was a newlywed. Very practical and down to earth, warm and smiling, when she moved into our building. In her early 30s, Priya got married to a guy she met in college. Deeply in love, both were coming to terms with their cultural differences, he being from an agricultural family in Bihar, and she from this women-only household, financially independent, Maharashtrian family based in Pune. There could not be two more different people. Being young, they soon moved to the Middle East to make some additional income. Both of them got jobs there, doing the 8.30 am to

5.30 pm routine, managing to save a fair bit, till their child was born. Priya decided to quit her job and look after the baby. In the Middle East, being a housewife on 20,000 Dirhams per month makes for a comfortable lifestyle.

The Middle East is a haven for aspiring youngsters with consumerist dreams. And there are well-appointed malls which offer an escape of a few hours for young mothers, with shopping, eating, entertainment and all sorts of pampering. You need weeks to finish exploring one mall. 'Homemaker' has a prestigious sound to it, to compensate for the loss of the professional designation.

But when they had to move back to India during an economic slowdown, the equation began to crumble. For the woman here, 'homemaker' (yes with small h) becomes an empty title. Because the same housework which was done by one cleaning lady in the Middle East who would visit twice a week for 2 hours per day, to clean house from top to bottom requires three persons now – a) the untrained house maid, who goes through the motions of cleaning; b) the housewife who follows her around to make sure that she cleans all the visible places, and c) the odd cleaning service company who comes on Diwali to clean what the maid and the memsahib have neglected to see under the furniture. And this is only as far as the cleaning is concerned. To describe other household tasks which forms the content of a housewife's job, will take me another chapter at least.

I am not making fun of all the silent workers who toil tirelessly, but want to take this opportunity to suggest that it is time, we turned essential services into organised companies whereby these jobs can be outsourced. This way not only will the workers get salaries and long-term benefits, they will also acquire the status of being respectable job-holders, with minimum wage and opportunities for promotion. Homemakers will have support. With proper training and certification, it will be a win-win for both.

To come back to Priya, the only free time she had now was the one spent in traffic. From an upcoming lawyer to housewife, the transition was visible in her demeanour. There was no symbol in the Indian social setup to acknowledge her contribution to her family. A girl who never needed to make herself a sandwich, had abandoned her law degree in favour of doing the house work 'to better care for her family'.

However much one could accept her desire to be the perfect housewife and mother, for me what was unpalatable was her husband's attitude. Speaking to her as if she was a dim-witted woman, in the presence of their child. In the Middle East, law enforcement protects the woman if her husband ill-treats her. But here? Society rewards the husband for keeping wife 'in line', making her cook and serve hot snacks, and food when friends come over for drinks. While he gets complimented for his hosting, she gets to add 'good cook' to her housewifely accomplishments.

This is what we do to ourselves – disconnect from our pain and anger. Join Yoga classes to try and find inner peace and balance but let go of our self-worth as architects or doctors, or lawyers and engineers.

Younger women tell me that things have changed now and girls can exercise more say in their lives. I thought so too till I started looking around at prospective brides and grooms for both my kids. Newspaper Ads showed me that nothing had changed since 1982 when my parents started looking for a suitable match for me.

When you read one Ad which says, 'very beautiful, fair, slim, Jat girl..... Haryanvi Jat boy settled' next to another

Wanted Groom		Wanted Bride
R.C.Goan girl 26/5'3" B.Sc, MBA, fair company's Manager, trustworth, expects suitable qualified intelligent, good personality value oriented	SUITABLE Match for very beautiful, fair, slim, Jat girl (Gotra Kadian Dangi Dalal) 23/ 5'-7", Pursuing M.A. English, B.Ed., Haryanvi Jat boy settled	✓ Gaur Brahmin Nm 26/ 5'8 Be/ 8- Lpa Working P (locl) Maharashtra Seeks Working Girl Pref. l 9033XXXXXX, 941XXXXXX
✓ Suitable match for Maha jan Girl, 5'-3", June 1983. Lecturer engineering college near Chandigarh. Upper caste no bar send particular.	Suitable Match for Hindu Sethi (Khatri) Girl (Non-Manglik) MA. Fair. Slim, Beautiful, 5'-3", September 13, 1987 (1:40 AM/ Chandigarh). High	Vinod jalan, dob: 05.06.1980, time: 7.05 pm, 5'10" fair, bansal, senior software engineer, 9lakh baran : 90XXXXXXXX,

Fig. 1

one which says '…girl, lecturer engineering college near Chandigarh … Caste no bar…' what conclusion does a normal person come to? That we have a good-looking slim daughter and therefore we will not compromise in our expectations, which is a boy from within the community; and those parents who don't have good looking daughters must educate their daughters and get them into good jobs and even after that we will settle for any boy who is willing to overlook her lack of looks. As for the boy, parents have decided that qualifications, salary and looks are enough to get him a good match. He gets to be him, but she has to compromise.

I logged on to marriage portals because after all I am an educated and an aware mother. Girls' profiles highlighted, 'I cook – Chinese, South Indian and Mexican. Follow family values… looking for a boy who respects family'. Boy's profile detailed his hobbies.

These are crucial transitions in life, when change in society's attitudes and values, *should* begin to be evident. It doesn't seem so, seeing that India is still the largest market for fairness creams and gold. In fact, the fairness criteria has been so successful, at least for marketeers, that they have started creating demand for fairness creams for men as well.

As a nation, are we so inured to a woman's pain that we are now teaching it as marketing strategy? Have the marketing professionals studied the impact fair skin has had on women's lives? My friend Beena was discarded by her husbands' family because of her dusky complexion. Today Beena is a Head Teacher of a Montessori school on a Hong Kong Island, where all parents swear by her skill as a teacher. Parents change the school of their child to make sure that they are taught by Beena. I'm sure statistics of women divorced due to dusky complexion is not available in the report which highlight revenues earned from fairness creams.

I don't blame marketeers for not exercising their conscience because money has no colour. But do we teach our children to have a conscience? Do we tell our girl children, 'you can be who you want to be'? Or that…but, your place is in the home.

I have the latest statistics from World Bank to show how India fares in women's participation in the labour market.

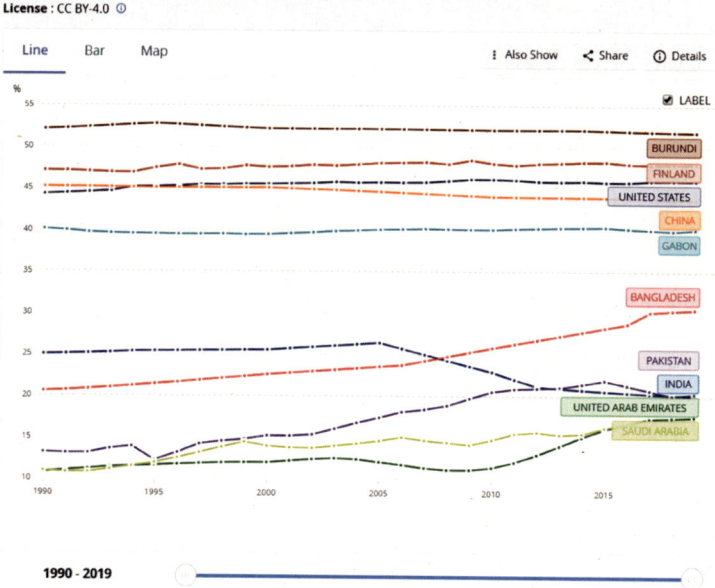

(Indian Express 8 March 2020). Fig 2: Worker Population Ratio (WPR) in usual status (ps+ss) for persons of age 15 years and above all-India.

These graphs clearly indicate that even though we see ourselves among the developed nations, but as far as the female* labour participation rate (FLPR) is concerned, we are equivalent to other nations in the region, eg the Middle East. Considering the restrictions on women that are in place, especially in Saudi Arabia, these figs reflect our slip. Even countries like Bangladesh, Gabon and China are higher than us. In India, the glass ceiling for women's career is India's glass ceiling.

Changing attitudes towards women's participation in the workforce is a national priority. *This requires a social change which cannot be achieved without changing attitudes in society.*

I have met many dads who gave wings to their daughters by educating them, but then clipped their wings by preferring marriage over career growth. I find girls settling for jobs offering very little pay rise just because they are nearer home, while boys shift cities in search of 'good prospects'.

All the double standards that are applied in society, I call them Magic Beans. I am sure all of you have heard the story of Jack and the Beanstalk? We bring up our children with these double standards and then expect Magic to happen.

Here are the details where the Magic Beans are taking women.

Act i – the Magic Beans

In my research sample, based on data available for 46 women, here is the distribution of women who left their jobs vs. those who didn't.

Research Findings:

i.i) In the age group 25–30 all the women were first line

---

* For Urban India it is 23% for females according to the PIB.
https://pib.gov.in/PressReleaseIframePage.aspx?PRID=1966154

managers; one was married and, for these women there were **zero career breaks**.

i.ii) As many as 67% of the women who had got married, had taken maternity leave at some point or another.

i.iii) Contrary to expectations, not all had left; some had even cut short their maternity leave to come back to work. In fact, 45% of married women who had not left their jobs, came back to the same job, immediately after maternity break or at some other point in their career. Case in point – **Farida Hussain**, who kept in touch with the company, to ensure that she could apply whenever a vacancy came up.

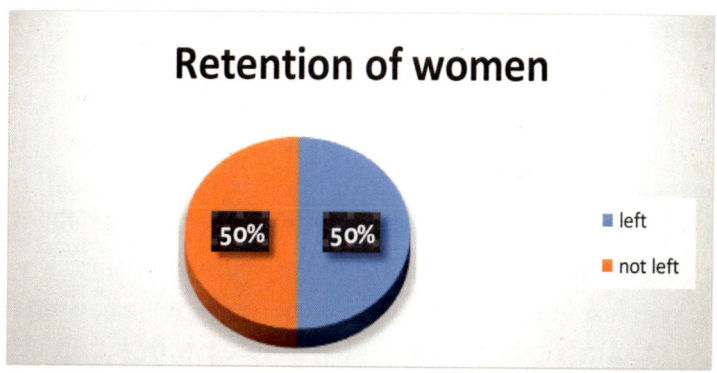

Fig 3

Before I go on, let me specify that I have not captured the exact age when break was taken because leave was taken in the past and age was not a critical factor. However, I can categorically state that the 22% who quit their jobs did so because of:

a. Health issues of the baby which necessitated devoting full time to child care;

b. Health issues of a close family member (father or mother etc);

c. Spouse relocated to another city or country;
d. Study leave for self.

Reasons c) and d) are not really impediments in a woman's career because spouse's relocation to another city has invariably been to a bigger metro or country, leading to better jobs for the women. A robust job market, better commuting facilities, and domestic support which has enabled women's return to an active workforce. Similarly, some used reason d) strategically to enhance qualifications – **Mukta Gogia** (B Tech from NIT), did an MBA during her maternity break. Some have also changed their profession, to match their new responsibilities. For example, **Dr Sindhu C S** moved from medicine to an administrative healthcare job. She requalified herself, did Master's in Hospital Administration from Tata Institute of Social Science, Mumbai, and a Diploma in Financial Management – 'So that I do not have night calls or shift duties. I am happy doing an administrative job'. She is currently heading Zon Healthcare Consulting Division.

i.iv) Just like the place where Jack threw the magic beans (in Jack and the Beanstalk) had a lot to do with the growth of the beanstalk overnight, location plays a large role in the career graph of a woman. It is not the culture of the city where she has grown up, but rather the city in which she is working that has an identifiable impact. The city (a specific city) where a respondent works has a specific set of conditions – security, transport, awareness, level of professionalism of co-workers, domestic support, male attitudes. That is why Aishwarya Joshi told me, 'I was the only woman architect on four different sites on Palm Jumeirah (UAE) for a duration of three years. I faced 900 to 1,500 men every day. I was told to behave like a man but I refused to do that and just behaved like myself, delivered the job as an individual and did what was required. I created leaders there who made my work easier and accepted me for who I was rather than for being the lady on site'.

On the other hand, a single lady in a real estate company in Gurgaon, India is not able to work even in a team with 15 male co-workers, because the latter are constantly ridiculing her for requesting co-workers to accompany her. Another lady in Kolkata joined a bigger company for growth, but came back to her previous company because her boss in the new company would call her to work on a Saturday, when the office was empty. This was despite the new company being a Multinational Company, with well-established procedures (the Vishakha Guidelines) to check harassment of women. They were able to get away, because nobody from head office wanted to travel to Kolkata to do an inspection of the actual state of affairs.

Other women pursued their hobby or started their own ventures as free lancers, teaching arts and crafts, or found some outlet for their talent. They come back with a renewed sense of direction and confidence. In fact, one of the mothers who rejoined, **Dr Jeroze Dalal**, free lanced as a consultant during her break, and is now the Strategic Business Unit head of Novartis. Shiba Maggon, the first woman in the history of Indian basketball to represent a country as a player, a coach and a referee, returned as a world-class coach and referee, not to forget the boxer Mary Kom, whose last international fight was in 2021, at age 39 and as a mother of four.

The question, therefore, is how to increase the number of women at the entry level so that the funnel can be enlarged and the reasons why women leave can be normalised.

In this scenario the role of government policy-makers is crucial by them specifying what is 'normal'. I have to look at on-ground cases in point. Recently when six months maternity leave was made mandatory for companies, I met Jignal two years after I had hired her for a client.

Jignal came from a middle-class family. When she got married, a year after I hired her, she was still working to support her parents because her brother was in his teens. When she was expecting her first child, she hid it from her employers, because by then the law regarding the mandatory 6-month maternity leave had already been passed. Her fears were not unfounded. As she was nearing her sixth month, her company's HR department came to know. Sure enough, at the next round of 'layoffs' she was asked to leave, as the company no longer needed trainers. Who cares about Jignal's financial plans – of putting her younger brother through college, helping parents with their livelihood? After all her income is 'pocket money'. Six months after the birth of her baby, Jignal was back at another job, commuting from Palghar (a suburb in Mumbai, India) to Andheri by train, only to continue supporting her parents. I wonder what was the punishment meted out to the company that fired her to avoid paying maternity pay.

Having to pay salary to Jignal during her maternity may form one of the reasons why 16% of the married women are forced to drop out by their employers. However, her love for her family is the overriding reason why 84% of the women come back to work after their maternity break.

Research Findings:

This phenomenon, of women falling through the cracks of the social system in India – between getting an education, joining the workforce, growing through the middle rungs of corporate career, and leaving before reaching a senior position

– is called the leaking pipeline, whereby the number of women lessens as the positions increase in seniority.

The 'Leaking Pipeline' has a sociological hypothesis, leaving fewer women in senior positions. Due to reasons and norms prevalent in the larger social structure, it leaves very few women candidates available for board level positions.

Qualification	Years of experience	Females	Total	Percentage
CA	0 to 5	8484	20000	42.42
CA	5 to 10	10246	20000	51.23
CA	10 to 15	5185	20000	25.925
CA	15 to 20	2142	20000	10.71
CA	20 TO 25	297	5287	1.485
CA	25 TO 30	137	3526	0.685
CA	30 TO 35	36	1450	0.18

The above fig shows the percentage of women Chartered Accountants available in the job market as against men. These are figures are from one job portal. The lowest percentage is of women CAs at experience level of 30 to 35 years, probably because there were lesser number of women studying Chartered Accountancy in the late 1980s. The percentage increases as experience level decreases – this reflects the number of women opting for CA as a profession. This reduction in availability of women candidates in positions of financial decision making, 'conspires' to leave male CAs as head of organisations.

The leaking pipeline has an economic impact. Chapter 2 explores reasons why 84% of the women come back after their maternity break. The author believes that reinforcing these will have a multiplier effect on the leaking pipeline.

Act ii – The Bonds of Sisterhood

Age 30-40 is seen as the period when a career peaks, both for men as well as women. To take a closer look at the trend in this age group, I divided the group into two: 30-35 & 35-40.

This is the age group where ideally, given capability, women should be at the department or business head level. My data showed that most of the married women had finished with their maternity/ study breaks. In the age group of 30–35, all the women were managers, or higher. In this category, father's illness and spouse relocation, were the major reasons for women dropping out.

Maximum career breaks were seen at age 35-40 onwards. The career cookie, for women, begins to crumble. Suddenly there seems to be a rush for the door. Family health, harassment at work, spouse relocation, changing career, own health were some of reasons cited. In this age group, for the first time I saw organisational factors emerge – sexual harassment and bullying.

Excluding maternity, reasons were:
Family – *caregiving /responsibilities at home, spouse relocating to another city, own health, marriage, and lack of family support.*
Organisation – *sexual harassment and unethical management.*
Career - *shifting gears, becoming entrepreneur and study leave.*

This seems to be the age group at which women are the most vulnerable – women begin to leave jobs to cope with family issues. At the same time, pressure mounts at work because of vertical growth. In the family, their presence being vital, their inability to give a 100% in both areas pushes them out of the system.

Her problem becomes her 'personal' problem and therein falls Rome.

This is the defining moment, the critical juncture, where a strong external factor, the current boss or an active women's group, or a personal coach can re-align her directions, anchor her in her professional aspirations.

Act iii – Shifting Gears

In the age group 40–50 in which over 30% of the respondents were included, one respondent left the corporate sector to become an entrepreneur, while two joined NGOs. Shifting gears in the later years (40+) of their lives, women have the satisfaction of having reached some level in their career and then decide to shift focus to things other than work, to find meaning in their lives.

Act iv – Stepping Out of the Room

My data on women showed that 32.5% of the respondents are now single – 50% of these (7 of 13) have remained single by choice, expressly to pursue a career. Some have been rendered single due to circumstances like death of the spouse or separation/divorce. This segment seems to be growing by the day.

The term 'stepping out of the room' signifies the increasing trend among young women to pursue a life of meaning vs marriage. It would be so easy to conclude that if women chose singlehood, their career will prosper. However, that does not solve the problem, because that carries with it its own set of misconceptions. As a society, are we doing enough for our daughter's financial self-reliance, keeping in mind this new reality?

Even though Hindu Succession Act lays down that the daughter has equal share in father's property as her brothers, there are loopholes in the implementation of the law which enables her male sibling to exclude her from inheritance. Similarly, a married woman has no right on her in-law's property, except what her husband decides to bequeath to her. Nor can she demand anything.

Therefore, it is imperative that women continue to pursue their career, in order to safeguard their financial future. This is not respondent Priya's problem alone. At some point of our journey, by keeping quiet, we have all created our 'bosses', by giving away the decisions of our lives. We have perpetuated the gender bias that victimises us – that fosters the notion that husbands make money, while working women make 'pocket money'.

The point now is what needs to change? Expecting that education alone will make a difference, is expecting too much. If we look at the educational background of my respondents, I find that 48% of the postgraduates were facing the same issues as PhDs, or Graduates (see chart below).

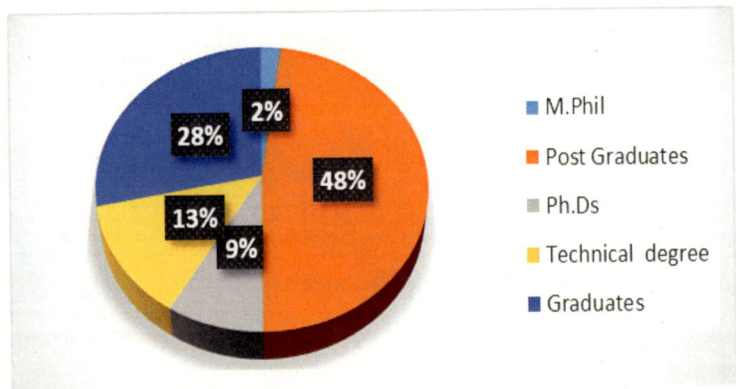

Fig 4

The only difference I saw was that PhD, Technical degree (professional for short) gave the women a different perspective of handling the challenges in their career. For eg., **Meenal Bhat** said, 'I gave up work because I was always tired. For about a year I was working part time; first as a consultant, with my previous company; then I started picking up projects from outside. I have my own company now'.

Research Conclusion

*This problem, of not acknowledging that women have to live with a different reality than that of men at the workplace, that they do **not** see the world as equal at the workplace, has been long overlooked.* We are nearing the completion of the first quarter of the 21st century. How many more years do we have to wait for the arena to be equalised?

When I say unequal, I am talking about the workplace terms that are defined with reference to males – rewards, policies, expectations, compensation and benefits, even behavioural competencies. Standards for all competencies like Initiative, Aggression, Assertiveness, Communication, Result Orientation, Team Orientation are defined with the Man in mind. But for a woman it may not be the standard.

In India, for women, the norm, or *Sanskar*, is 'keep quiet'. So does that mean she has no initiative? There are some norms a woman has to relearn when she joins the workforce.

Trapped in an economy that doesn't encourage them to 'speak up' and expects nothing more from them than showing up every day, not making their presence felt, the workplace becomes another exploitative institution. Doing low-paying jobs, with no social security, moving from company to company for a few hundred rupees and a train pass, these women are the invisible workers dotting the SME sector. Too educated to need empowering by an NGO, too proud to ask family for help, and not earning enough to afford an adequate support system for herself…. Workplace becomes another disempowering place.

At home, the woman is familiarised with the culture by her mom or mom-in-law, and the consequences of not following them are clearly explained. But in the corporate sector she has to assume. Nothing is clearly spelt out, the woman has to learn by making mistakes while the men laugh at her discomfiture. There is that constant fear of making a mistake, without knowing what the mistake is. This is one piece that is missing for which the consequences are severe on her career.

So dense is this piece, that even Satya Nadella, CEO of Microsoft fell prey to it. When asked how women should go about asking for a raise, his response was that, 'it's not really about asking for a raise, but knowing and having faith that the system will give you the right raise. Doing so is an act of good karma, of knowing that the rewards will eventually come back to you'.

Telling women that you will get an engineering degree if you do the hard work, but getting a raise is 'their karma', then aren't we perpetuating double standards? While women in America took Nadella to task for his remarks, can women professionals in India demand an apology from their CEO?

CHAPTER 2

REWRITING TRADITIONAL ROLES

EDUCATION IN AN Indian household has always been considered vital, sometimes placed even before subsistence needs. Knowledge develops the mind and is treated not only as a means to acquire an income but as a means of scholarship, excelling in music and arts, trade, or spiritual enlightenment for some. We were a knowledge-based economy long before the word became fashionable. And that is what encouraged the scientific temper. The *guru* was the means to salvation. Even though professions were hereditary, the sons had to learn and work hard to earn their place next to the father, on the seat which signified the profession. The loom, the pundit's seat, the musical instrument, the chopdi (account books) all occupied a place of devotion. These were worshipped on Lakshmi Puja day. The father was the CEO of the profession, besides being head of the family and it was incumbent upon him to maintain the professional standard. If the son did not measure up to the standards, another industrious student would be trained to take up the profession/business. Students came from far and wide to learn the trade from proponents of arts, crafts, music. The only gap from today's perspective was that daughters were not inducted into the family business (more on this later). If a family had the means, daughters were educated up to the level they desired. Women could choose their own partners, who they felt were equal to them in intellectual ability, beauty and *sanskara,* like Ram and Sita.

A career, too is built within an industry or a function, on experience of a very deep nature; the depth of experience comes from a wide variety of exposures within that industry, handling different kind of crises, territories, which is an investment the women have to make to acquire the required capability.

Let us look at how some of the successful women in my research sample built their capabilities.

a. A Mission to Return

Whenever women have gone back to their old jobs, it is because they had to deal with a particular problem, or fulfill a business need, or meet a challenge. They responded to the challenge and jumped back into the fray because it was close to their heart and took their life in the desired direction. This fact was common irrespective of whether they worked in a community, family, institution or organisation.

Whether it was Gurpreet Wadhera's desire to support her husband in launching his product, or it was Jeroze Dalal's desire to become the MD of a clinical research company, or **Pooja Arora's** desire to give alternate therapy a chance, or Neela Satyanarian's drive to be an IAS officer, the fact is that their mission was like a bee in their bonnet. It is not that they didn't have domestic commitments; they managed their domestic situation with an overall focus on their mission. Their ability to create the infrastructure at home *first,* in order to support their objectives spelt the difference between success and failure on both fronts.

Problems are the petri dish in which leadership thrives!

It was only when women were in a critical business function and had made significant contributions to the business or the key operations that they emerged as leaders. Be it sales, business development, operations, commercial or hardcore reporting; their mettle became more visible when they made a noticeable difference to a critical factor impacting ***business***. This applies to the leaders who head voluntary organisation as well. This is a wonderful facet of 'mom bosses', which clearly demonstrates the difference a mother makes to industry when she leaves for work every day.

Whether it is Elizabeth Sen, Farida Hussain, Tasneen Padiath, Managing Director of CEB South East Asia, or Sally Holkar, they surmounted the challenge, chose to win the client over with their knowledge and contribute to the bottom line. Leaders believe in action and the issue becomes the framework for driving their actions and decisions.

Once inside the office, there is no difference in what a man has to do or what a woman has to do. The goal post is the same for all. How each of us tackle the ball on the field determines the outcome. And because more often it has been the masculine style in professions, male characteristics have become synonymous with getting work done. As more women take up the financial mantle in their households, the gender preference for business leadership roles will disappear.

We hope!

b. High Learning Desire

Many women have the desire to learn from challenges and people; my conversations centered on what they had learnt from challenges and how they applied the lessons learnt. To them, the problem was an opportunity to test their conceptual understanding of the situation. It tested the courage of their conviction, which became the *fulcrum* of their leadership. Invariably, the outcome was a more optimistic approach.

Investing in career growth through networking, attending conferences or learning new skills is just another part of their daily schedule. Time is not compartmentalised but spent equally at both places – home and work; for example, they practice tools and techniques learnt at work, at home like chore delegation with children, appreciation techniques or decision-making. They have changed their lifestyle to make work-life balance their key focus.

Let's take a look at how **Rohini Venkatesh**, Sr Assurance Advisor with RSM US LLP, planned her learning path. In her words, 'I took risks. Most of us tend to stay in our safe environment/zone because of our cultural experience, which is poisonous for us. I did not settle for this safe zone, I had desires. I also had the fear of giving up my job, on which depended my financial independence, therefore, I took a route where I could balance both work and home. I took the risk of giving up my mainstream job (above the age of 40). I then looked for opportunities to get different kinds of jobs, where I could acquire specific skills. I had integrity and no apprehensions about taking up different kinds of jobs. For example, I learnt how to operate computers, since programming was becoming a key skill required by the industry. I could rip apart the computer and fix it – my growing passion for technology opened up a whole new world for me.

'A big chunk of the transition was my own perception of who I am; at that point my self-image was very negative. I did not feel good about being treated the way I was by people because of an inferiority complex about my looks and lack of money. I needed self-awareness to be realistic about my strengths and drawbacks. It was a self-driven journey, which was built up within me by talking to people who helped me deal with my inner demons.

'I grew in the organisation by building on my skills. What governed me was that I should work hard, not dress smart. I would talk to people a lot about my desire to do a challenging job, till one day somebody heard me; she was a marketing person. She recommended me for an executive's role and one of my bosses allowed me to take up managerial responsibilities, which gave me exposure to negotiate and analyse. This helped me build experience.

'Once I moved to the US, I started from scratch. I acquired the degree required to start a career here. Since I'd had the experience of switching or starting new careers in the past, I decided to pursue corporate financial management here, which included both accounting and finance. It helped that there was less stigma abroad, of what a woman should and shouldn't do. People do any odd jobs to make money, be it to secure a future for themselves or education. The culture there is not based on **stereotyping**.'

Aishwarya Joshi did a certification course from Singapore once she decided to become a Corporate Social Responsibility (CSR) practitioner. Pooja Arora, a BE, MBA from XLRI, after giving up her cushy Regional Brand Manager job in P&G Singapore, spent two years learning Reiki, Ayurveda, Yoga, massage therapies, employment laws in Singapore and a coaching certification. This comes with, in Pooja's words, 'Envisioning – taking the idea or the project and making it really big and attractive to sell it to people.'

As against this, if we were to look at the careers which

stalled, I saw some women who gave up because they thought they had no other choice. This fact was brought out repeatedly in the interviews. This was the ***critical differentiator***.

Once a woman starts a family, most of them retreat into the default traditional set of beliefs of being a 'good' wife or daughter-in-law. The problem is compounded by the fact that training for most courses often involves overnight stay. Typically, women progress in their managerial role during 28–35 years of age, which is also the age when most women have children. Often women let the professional challenges go by, prioritising their children's academic development over their own.

From this perspective, gender equality is not just about ***giving*** equal rights to women. In fact, it is a barrier, a breach in intended equality. A giver has an upper hand, and the receiver, lower. Thus, 'giving' freedom' destroys the very concept of equality and bestows superiority to the so-called giver and renders the receiver, inferior. Freedom cannot be given; it has to be earned with intent and energy.

c. Meaningful Life

Meaning is very personal. For Pooja Arora based in Singapore it is, 'Alternate natural health and well-being. I had an accident when I was 20, which led to a broken neck and spine. It took 5 to 6 years of physiotherapy for the bones to set. However, I have spent last 15 to 16 years battling the injury using alternate methods like yoga, Reiki and Ayurveda. So I would feel satisfied if I dabble in that.'

For Mukta, 'I was influenced by my father being in an authoritative position and opted for a professional career. I worked for almost 2 years in the R&D department of a textile mill in Ludhiana, Punjab. But I soon realised that it was not for me. Textile mills were majorly dominated by men and most of the work was around managing labour. I was the only female in a senior role and these mills were far away from the city. I wanted to work in a more innovative environment that gave me freedom to experiment as I was technology oriented; that would have made my efforts more meaningful and utilised my knowledge.'

Nupur Sood, AVP-Ad Sales, Colors says, 'There are lots of things pending in my to-do list. I want to get into a national media agency once my kids are a little settled, I want to travel to certain places, pursue dance once again and look forward to taking care of my grandchildren eventually. I'm planning and securing a future for that.'

As for me, I set up my own consultancy, to find 'people-led' solutions for problems in the workplace.

So, now I don't shy away from the knocks life gives me. I may shed a few tears, but hidden behind them is another message – that I need to change; what I need to change may take time to figure out but I welcome the process. I have learnt to separate the emotion from such incidents by using dispassionate words, removing the 'you' and the 'I' and the 'feeling' from the conversation, leaving my gender at home, yet operate from my core strengths.

d. Desire to Achieve

Aspirations were a huge part of what drives most women. Elizabeth Sen advises, 'You have to be really selfish about your aspirations if you want to progress. An organisation exists as an environment – put your own milestones in place, it's for you to figure out what you want – that's the magnet.'

Tasneen Padiath says, 'I have learnt over time that if you don't ask for it, you don't get it, so don't be afraid of asking.

Last year, I took on a very challenging role. I was head of sales for a business unit that was not doing well and my boss told me that either I will do really well and will be promoted or I am going to end up in disaster. He said that whatever I was going to do, that I should do it with my eyes open. It was a very challenging role and involved a lot of travel, which I had not done at all for three years as I was focused on the kids. However, at that juncture, I thought, either I decide to go ahead full steam or completely step back. I took on the challenge and, thankfully, it turned out well, I was promoted, but it could have gone the other way as well. A lot of hard work… lot of travel… not seeing my children. Nevertheless, yes, I managed to rise to the occasion! But it would not have been possible without family support, for that was the key. Before I took on the role, I discussed the matter with my husband like always. For instance, last year he took on a role, which was easier for him in a way, it was a trade off on his side. We had talked about it beforehand. Similarly, three years ago, he was travelling and I was looking after the children. In the last year or so, he took on a different type of role which did not involve travelling and thus it helped me a lot. My mother also was a great help. She lives in Kerala but last year she spent a lot of time with my children. This was how I handled the crises. They were with the children even if I was not.'

Vasanthi has to say, 'While many organisations give new mothers pick-up and drop facility, I want to tell women not to wait for anyone to make this arrangement for you. As an organisation, if you are gender-friendly, then give all your employees equal opportunities but be sensitive enough to give women extra care. How can I work in the night shift is not a question for the organisation to answer; why accept the offer if you're unhappy with it? Therefore, solve that problem on your own and move on.'

In stark contrast to this conversation were other conversations, which hovered around reasons why women did not want to take the leap – because it would have called for something they were not willing to give up on, be it their beliefs or love for their family. The reason, however, was found to be in the external environment.

The fight is not 'without', it is 'within'. The point is not whether the glass ceiling exists; the point is that we believe it exists, outside of us.

e. Taking the Leap

Among the women I spoke to, I found there was a difference in perspective on what they considered as a challenge. Those who have successfully reached a level of leadership mention an issue in business operations as the challenge, while women who have not fulfilled their destiny, spoke of personal challenges.

If I was to analyse the different challenges faced by the respondents in this study, I see that the challenge emerged at three different levels.

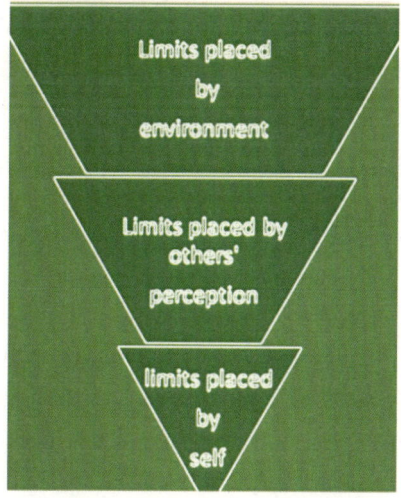

Fig 5

Limits placed by one's own self involve doing things you have not done hitherto like travelling, night shifts or working late. Of course, it involves ensuring that your employer has taken proper measures to ensure safety and security. If the employer has not made such an arrangement, then it is up to you to align with other decision-makers in the company and ensure these minimum safety measures are put in place. Fight for these rather than leaving on time, because it is beneficial to all. Be your own protector.

Limits placed by other's perception are when you allow other's beliefs to become your roadblocks. Then you are as much to blame for perpetuating the assumption that you need protection. This is how **Nandini Goswami**, Head of Corporate Communications for an MNC based in Mumbai handled it. 'When I first started working, I was a crime reporter with *Hindustan Times*. There was a murder in a red-light area and my boss didn't want to let me go. He said a woman mustn't go there. I didn't give up. I said if I was a crime reporter, have gone to several crime scenes, seen bodies and am strong enough to do that, why can't I go for this story? I managed to convince him and go there. Women very often give up. But because I didn't, I not only got a very good story but wrote a great article because I provided a woman's insight to the story too.'

If you want to move ahead in your career, then don't expect others to make concessions for you. Check whether the perception the other person has about you is based on fact or a feeling. Take action to dispel that perception. This has a major impact on how your subordinates and peer group perceive you –as an equal and not somebody needing protection.

Farida Hussain recalls, 'I remember my first meeting; I was speaking like a school teacher. So many people pulled my leg for it, since I was able to answer their questions. However, I knew it'll be okay. Everybody will test you; every time people don't know you, they will test you. So you have to ensure you are very good, in fact, much better than good!'

The third level limits are the beliefs and stereotypes held in the public domain – such as, 'A friend of mine from college, married into a joint family in Delhi and is tortured by her mother-in-law who insinuates that she is having an affair, whenever she gets late due to a traffic jam,' or 'Let's hire North Indian women for business development roles,' or, 'Let's not hire newly-married women because they will take leave for sure.' Though there is not much you can do about these as it involves the general public, there have been women who have surmounted this challenge too. This is possible with training and mentoring on how to bring out these biases at the interview, or by networking with other working women. Your grasp of your subject has to be so sound that all these gender factors become irrelevant.

Farida shares her experience: 'At social networking sessions, if you don't want to be part of that type of networking, then you have to develop other types, which should compensate. I have never been part of binge meetings or meeting customers; however, it never affected me because I focused on bettering myself at my work. So there were never any complaints on the work front. Even when the customer would want to socialise, I was clear that I would connect with them through my work skills rather than social skills.'

Tasneen: 'I have faced gender biases more externally, with clients and their members. Though my work is advisory in nature, sometimes when I walk into a client's place, they do not want to take advice from a woman. I face those multiple times not only in Asia but also in the United States. I have been in markets which are very tough for women – Ohio and Texas have a male-dominated culture. Advice from an Asian, and especially from a woman, it is not very well received here. All this I have experienced externally but never internally.

'(Overcoming) It came with time. I was interacting with these clients for over two years and demonstrating my expertise. The first few interactions were not easy but by demonstrating my expertise in my domain, they started trusting me. They started seeing me not as an Asian or a woman but as somebody who can help them address their issues. Therefore, you just have to work to gain client's trust. Of course, there are people with prejudices you cannot overcome but, at the end of the day, you are working towards the same outcome or objective as they are. You walk the talk and show them that you can provide value; then it becomes a much more professional interaction.'

Prachi, an HR professional from Delhi: 'My challenge is getting people to understand that deadlines lead to hurry – getting leaders to accept that is what I am working towards. When they see the fallout, they are more accepting next time of the initiatives that we want to undertake at my company to ensure that employees are happy. Every time there is a leader that connects with a team, their results are more productive.'

I am sharing these instances here so that anybody can use these tips to overcome other's perception, prejudices, and perceptive beliefs, whether glass or steel. It is not a state of matter proposition like the ozone layer or black hole, it is a belief! Fortunately, the best thing about glass is that it is breakable.

You can believe everything that *you want to* believe.

May be a family member or stranger, the point is not who draws the line, but that a woman stays within the line – the proverbial *Lakshman Rekha*. This concept crept into *Tulsidas's*

Ramayana only in the sixteenth century, all the many previous *Ramayanas*** had no such thing as a 'Lakshman Rekha' for women; it was adopted by societies and cultures in this subcontinent only in the medieval times. Today, this line is so deeply embedded in the psyche of the Indian woman that she does not even question the validity of the line and carries its stigma everywhere.

The Lakshman Rekha, as most of us know, was a mythical line drawn by Lord Ram's brother Lakshman for Sita to indicate the decorum she needs to follow while they were away. The Lakshman Rekha implied, and still does, the duties and responsibilities of being a wife, daughter and mother. It is supposed to be a measure of protection by males.

I am confident that this awareness will give women the confidence to identify *where is it they have drawn their own lines*. Not any Lakshmans. It is time to redraw the line, based on what women want – safety, achievement, values, expectations, well-being and priorities.

The Lakshman Rekha also has two interpretations – that Ravana or any male for that matter has no power inside the line, unless we give them the permission! To expand this interpretation further, classically it would mean that the man has drawn the 'Lakshman Rekha' to define his own limits, this far and no more. However, this expanded interpretation is never acknowledged in the patriarchal contemporary Indian societies.

The day we see the limitless blue sky beyond the glass ceiling, the Lakshman Rekha becomes a stepping-stone in our journey to touch the sky.

** *Ramayana, A Comparative Study of Ramkathas*: A A Manvalan, Translators C T Indra & Prema Jagganathan, Vitasta Publishing, Delhi.

Before you dismiss this as a simplistic suggestion, let me remind you of all the leaders, inventors, entrepreneurs, creators, and sportsmen who started out with nothing more than talent few believed in, dedication and commitment to their goals. Their belief and the consistent hard work broke the ceiling placed by limiting beliefs held by others.

I am not decrying the glass ceiling effect, which is encountered by most women who have plateaued in their career due to gender-based beliefs. All that I am saying is – that as more and more women break these barriers and impact their external reality, the line itself will get redefined. Or reinterpreted as a line for men rather than women. Actions speak louder than words. The glass ceiling is another's perception, the other's stereotypical belief. My ceiling is my decision.

Take this book, for example, every time I was near a self-assigned deadline, I would always find excuses for not completing. The voice in my head would say, 'Just get two more interviews or some interview from east India, the United States or the United Kingdom, so that it is global, comprehensive, credible and exhaustive'. Actually, the 'more' is just an excuse to justify the lack of belief in what I have to say. The excuse is 'ab-out' and the tools to conquer are 'within'.

f. Managing a Team

Coming back to our original point about why 84% of the women I talked to came back to their jobs, is that they had been managing a team. The women leaders I spoke to are responsible for not only their own but also a team's performance. Their approach is to grow their team members' talent. Most leaders I spoke to wear this like a second skin, they enjoy making life wonderful, easier, and happier for their teams. This is 'how' they lead and connect with their teams.

There is no weak or strong team member; there are only tests for their leadership skills. The conversation flowed around developing people and that is how they *measured* their own leadership impact. They live by the same rules that they set for their teams.

'How to manage a team' was not something most of them studied or attended programmmes on; most of the managerial skills were acquired intuitively, perhaps an outcome of their personal observation of their role model's style during their formative years or first jobs. A few of them have shared their mantra for successfully managing teams in their interviews.

Dr Sindhu says, during one of her crisis management moments, 'Mobilising staff from different categories and making them multitask is required. I made technicians do the job of attendants and told nursing staff to help technicians; sweepers were helping to shift patients, which is actually the job of an attendant. Fortunately, hospital culture is such that patient service comes before anything else. So I just made them understand the situation. At that point there was no gender agenda, only a crisis which required everybody to chip in.'

Ad Sales Head for Colors, Delhi, Nupur Sood believes that the line starts from where she stands. 'For my team, I like to define expectations at the very onset, leaving no room for ambiguity. My principle is, "be honest and expect honesty". Trust me, this makes managing a team so much easier. And never ignore the fun element in anything anyone does. For me, work has never been a place where I have to go and swipe a card. Targets are set as per company expectations so that is a given, but the means to achieve those targets is what I go about setting and that everyone knows. So to me, achieving a number is not so important as the means and the effort in doing so, which is what I tell my team.'

In an interesting aside on the gender composition of the team, it was found that the percentage of males in business function teams tended to be more, ranging from 50% to 100% while teams in support function tended to have more women. Additionally, leaders in business functions tended to have larger teams ranging from 20 to 200+ (including indirect reports) while those in support functions tended to have smaller teams, 8 to 29. Needless to say, handling large teams requires greater competency as it is critical to career growth.

g) The 'people' Leaders

Their reason for taking responsibility of the team was always personal, for e.g. Sally Holkar, Zelma Lazarus and Pooja Arora rose as leaders in the social sector in response to requests made by people who were close to their heart. Their professional background gave them a means to channelise what they care about to a larger audience, in a structured manner. Research shows that for women, 'Gut feelings are not just emotional states but actual physical sensations that convey meaning to certain areas of the brain. The number of cells available in a woman's brain makes her extra receptive to track body sensations.' Call it sixth sense, premonition or forecasting, what you will but it does exist, say scientists.

This intuitive ability to catch emotional cues is the key to their emotional strength. Here are some excerpts from the interviews to support my observation:

Shiba Maggon has played in five FIBA Asian Championships for Women and was ranked in the top 5 for Asian players in 2002, a tall order for a woman who did not want to play basketball. 'A couple of people inspired me – my elder sister, Shelly Maggon who was a basketball player, we lost her in an accident. My dad then wanted me to pursue her dream, but mom helped me more to pursue it. She wanted me to be best player of the country and be on the winning team. She saved money for me to buy my shoes and helped me financially. She used to stitch clothes for people. I would say I did it for my sister and mother.'

As coach of the junior national basketball team, she helps her team manage their personal lives as well, because the students are still at a formative age. 'I have helped my students understand more about life. Most of them trust me more than they trust their parents and always take my advice in dealing with certain situations. I guess it's the way they are brought up. In the starting, they act very shy and don't talk to each other. But then, after a week, things get normal for them as I make it clear that they are not boys and girls but players and should act like that. When they see their coach behaving in a friendly manner, they start picking that up.'

According to **Zelma Lazarus**, Founder Impact Foundation 'Let me start with a little motto which my people follow: I shall pass by this way but once. Any good that I can do let me do it now, let me not defer or neglect it for I shall not pass this way again. This is the mission.

The working motto is SYNO, 'Stick your neck out'. Just go; what is the worst you can get? And NO-next opportunity.

'So that's the story of how we got on, and did amazing things. As a leader I do nothing. My team does the work and I get the praise. It is their project, not mine. Ownership is very important. Let each one feel it is my project. There is a very interesting story about where I learnt it. We were doing the polio-free Madras project. 300,000 children to be immunized. 1 child every 3 minutes. The very beloved Chief Minister was MGR. So I asked him if he would announce the project on TV. MGR was standing and next to him the Health Minister and me. He spoke in Tamil which I couldn't understand. All the while he was speaking, pointing like this (finger pointing inward) towards me. In the morning there was a write up in the newspaper about the project where he said that this is our project… we will make this State polio free and we will be the first State to be so, Sometimes you will see this lady, it is not her project. That's where I learnt Leadership. Anyone who comes forward, who lives on the street and says I want my child to be covered, I will give a certificate signed by me. That's the secret of the success of this project. In a time where every 3 minute a child was born, where national percentage of immunization was 25% in Tamil Nadu it was 92%. The United Nations has an annual report and gives one page report per country. That year the one page on India was the Tamil Nadu project. Zelma did nothing, She was there. Everybody said it is my job. That is the secret of where we are here today… just SYNO.'

According to Jeroze Dalal, who is now Global Trial Programme Head at Novartis, 'If you want to succeed, you have to be one with your team. Who is a leader? One who leads the team but the distance between them and the team should not be too wide. These things came with observation. At the same time, a woman must not be so strong that people are intimidated by her. I respect each and every team member, I acknowledge that each has a strength and weakness; as a manager my job is to pick out their strength and utilise those strengths. I'll give them those jobs where their talents can be projected, and that judgment is mine.'

CHAPTER 3

A WOMAN'S WORLD

ACCORDING TO HISTORIAN and author Arthur Llewellyn Basham's *The Wonder that was India*, 'A woman, according to most authorities, was always a minor at law. As a girl she was under the tutelage of her parents, as an adult, of her husband, and as a widow, of her sons. The *Arthashastra* reveals the restrictions that were imposed on women in Vedic times.

'And most of the role models of that time were women who were faithful and obedient to their husbands. However, she was treated with honor and accorded respect due to her. In later times, women sometimes took part in war.'

Women's roles have been primarily that of a nurturer and caregiver of the family. History shows that the Indian women who fought on the battlefields did so mainly to protect their husbands and sons. Rani Lakshmi Bai rose as a fighter during the Indian Rebellion of 1857; Razia Sultan (1205-1240) and Sarojini Naidu rose during the freedom struggle, highlighting the personal element, in 1947.

The age of science brought with it Janaki Ammal Edavaleth Kakkat, a botanist who researched cytogenetics and geography; and the organic chemist, Darshan Ranganathan.

The past gives birth to the future and, therefore, *to script a new way of 'being' for the Indian woman, we have to understand what is not working in the social constructs of the past.* In modern-day parlance, as the architect-entrepreneur Raylynne D'Sa puts it, 'According to me, Indian cultural influences on leadership would be the patriarchal male domination and lack of drive in women to change this imbalance due to a mental apathy and a make-do attitude with socially defined roles handed down generation after generation, that seem to have worked, at least on the surface. Yes, this would mean deferring the final say or "bigger share" or prime importance to the father or husband.' Or in the working space, 'the male boss'.

There is a huge gap between the goals of education and socialisation for Indian women. Why do things turn out differently than the goal for some women? I share some case studies here. These point to a more realistic role and a gender identity which enables their participation in society and economy in a constructive way.

I - Family Support

i. **Shilpi Kapoor**, Founder of Barrier Break Solutions Pvt Ltd is an Accessibility & Assistive Technology Expert and a Social Entrepreneur who focuses on creating technology for people with disabilities. Her vision is to change the way web is experienced by the physically challenged.

This gutsy and inspiring woman, a polar opposite of her saree-clad persona, says that, 'My granddad was my first role model. I admired his quality of doing things for others, guiding people, risk-taking, and the need to try what other people had not. He was truly a pioneer. Largely, I use his style, but also a lot of what I have seen in my parents. I was also influenced by my ex-boss. It was only after two years of working with him that I came to know he was paralysed, as we used to work together through the internet. With the use of technology, he overcame challenges. He used head tracking and sip-n-puff technology for doing difficult jobs. He never looked for sympathy. I guess I have learnt from them to take risks and try out new ideas. That is why I probably have managed to do what I do.'

'In our culture, biases stem from the family itself', Shilpi explains 'I see a lot of reluctance by families to invest in their daughters' businesses. But my parents have been very supportive. Most people wondered why my parents backed me the way they did; and my elder sister. They extended help not only emotionally but financially as well.'

In this case, the family support helped build confidence and self-esteem.

What happens in cases where this is neglected?

Dr Srabani Mukherjee, a Scientist E at the National Institute for Research in Reproductive Health, where she is focused on advancing the understanding of polycystic ovary syndrome and working towards deciphering newer pathways for improved treatment of its associated fertility. She chose a career in research as that is the environment in which she grew up, 'I come from a highly educated family. My mom and all my aunts are Master's degree holders in science and one of my uncles is a scientist with 29 patents to his credit. My mother was from the biology field, human physiology. She wanted me to be a doctor, but I was keen only on pursuing biological sciences. After MSc Biology, I completed a PhD fellowship. Observing them, I decided that I will never leave my job, whatever job it may be or if I have to leave, I will do something of my own.

'Secondly, I have seen two brilliant careers go down due to commitments at home. My mother was a college lecturer and was pursuing her PhD in the afternoons. She tried to continue her doctoral studies but had to leave midway due to my sister's ill health, as she could not afford a maid. First, she left her PhD and after a few years, she left her lecturer's job as well.

'Today, however, I face a similar situation. I may not be a very good administrator, but I have always wanted to be the director of my institute. Frankly speaking, I have to let go of that dream, as I have a lot of responsibility at home. I have to concentrate on my daughter, mom, and in-laws. I do not have much support at home and do not have much ambition at this stage. The majority of women who are climbing up the corporate ladder have family support, a joint family who share the responsibility. I am not from Mumbai, so I do not have concrete support here. In Kolkata it would have been a different story', she continues.

'In the field of science, it is said that you should not have any wife or husband because science is a 24-hour job and it is difficult to divert from it to manage home or personal life. This sums up my challenges in a nutshell. When I need to finish a paper or a grant, I take work home during the weekend. But home too needs attention. Sometimes, I feel guilty when I see other families taking their children for extracurricular activities. I have a nanny, but she is old and cannot take my daughter anywhere. What I want is help in running the house on a daily basis and have someone responsible who can have a hold on my child. My daughter is learning only from the nanny and I cannot help it.'

As a young woman, while doing her research abroad as a Junior Faculty position in the US at MD Andersen – one of the best Cancer Research Institutes in America, Mukherjee had to return to Mumbai to join her husband. She could have never foreseen this problem. Abroad, domestic services available are expensive but provided by trained people, who are accountable. However, this is not the case in India. With every middle-class household there are at least 3 to 4 service providers attached, but can we hold them accountable?

No doubt, families being the essence of Indian society, perpetuation of family norms become the overriding decision point. Women's life-changing decisions – education, marriage, starting a family, career become 'family' decisions rather than 'individual' or financial decisions. In most cases, even though joint families have ceased to exist, the reference point is parental preferences, because we live in a patriarchal society; that's how the music gets played.

II - Commercial Orientation

The women currently heading a business or driving a Profit Centre are the ones who have been habituated to earning their own living from a very young age. Attraction towards business is an interest which probably developed during their childhood. Their desire to be in a position of authority was nurtured by family members. Career choices sprang from what the women were attracted towards, not woven around 'what a woman is supposed to do'. Their self-identity was based on role models observed and processed within the real environment. Expressing their identity may have taken some time; however, their path came from a place of confidence.

ii. **Gurpreet Wadhera** is the GM & Co-Founder of Top Careers and You, based in Ludhiana. As a co-owner of the largest online student base in the country for exam preparations, covering 60+ exam categories, Gurpreet says, 'In fact, no one inspired me during my childhood. I belong to a business family where I saw my grandfather was very authoritative – I used to admire his wisdom, the way he earned money and earned respect in society. He owned a timber store, saw mill and flour mill, and also did fabrication of iron and steel. My grandmother was simple and quiet; a homemaker basically. Since childhood, I enjoyed being authoritative, or maybe it was my dream to be an independent person and (while) watching him, this desire developed in me.

'I am very straightforward and clear in my thoughts about my life. If people play games with me, I cannot tolerate it. Once, all my four team members went on leave. Actually, I fired one of the team members who lied to me in order to take leave. So, the rest of them protested by not turning up… but somehow it was a blessing in disguise. I was the only one handling my Centre from 7 am to 8 pm for two weeks at a stretch. I took that as a challenge and managed it successfully. That made me even stronger and gave out a strong message that lying will not be tolerated.

'It was my determination that helped me pull through. This is a quality I have possessed since the time I was teaching in college.' Gurpreet's story reflects that left to themselves; children will have gender independent role models. The work ethic inculcated in them from childhood – they were taught not to knead the dough, but earn the dough.

iii. **Elizabeth Sen,** the Deputy MD of APCO Worldwide, UAE, recalls her experience, 'I was also deeply influenced by my father who was from Kerala; he was the first person to move out of his village. He joined BHEL as an office clerk and worked till the age of 42. Then he started his own business, employing 200 people, all from his own village. And each family member was deeply involved in the business – labelling and packing and would stay up all night to ensure an order is completed on time. That urge to contribute through hard work was something I learnt from him.'

In this case, the commercial initiation was given by male members. What happens in cases where it is given by female members?

v. **Shivani Sharma,** Training Specialist at Amazon reveals, 'I am greatly inspired by my *nani jee* (grandmother) Asha Sharma, a business woman. In 1965 she took over her husband's garment business. She got married when she was 18 to my grandfather, T L Sharma, who was then 21 years old. Both of them were from middle-class families and their marriage was arranged. One day, my grandfather asked, "Asha, I am all alone, how will I run a business? I do not have any siblings or business partner." My nani smiled and said, "I am not only your wife; I am your business partner, source of support and love that every other relative can offer". This statement actually gave my grandfather courage to start a business without money or proper education.

'At that time, people were so orthodox that they wouldn't allow any woman to gain education or work, let alone run a business. My nani, along with her other household responsibilities, went for English tuitions so that she could learn to type business letters and attend business meetings. She worked till the age of 65. My mom, Veena Sharma, carried their legacy forward as a business woman. I used to sit with her after school and attend to customers, since I was in Class 5. That's when I began learning customer service skill and how to be a good leader because handling a team with many employees is no joke. I was always passionate about receiving and imparting training in various fields of business.'

These are tough women, who have learnt to thrive in the world of commerce. Recently, Shivani had to turn to freelancing because her child is small and flexi-work is not possible for trainers in her company.

III - Building Self-Worth

In families where daughters have been encouraged to define their own path, outside of a marriage, they have mostly ended up taking more risks with their capability.

vi. The person that comes to mind first and foremost is **Neela Satyanarayan.** 'I wouldn't have been able to do anything without my family. I gave up a degree and training programme from abroad and a posting in Delhi because I couldn't take my child. Apart from that, I have no regrets. My family has been my greatest support. My father taught me how to channelise the spiritual power of "Believe in yourself; you are answerable to yourself first, then to others." I have faced some very tough situations but I stood my ground because of that spiritual power.

'The quality my father inculcated in me didn't diminish even when reality hit, or upon interaction with others. It taught me that while most people wish to fraternise with or serve the high and mighty in society, I had been given the power to serve the common man. I never forgot this goal because my father taught me that I was "meant for them". I always got placed in these sectors. The common man gave me strength and courage to stand up and gave me insight in life. I have visited villages and mingled with many people. I feel it is a great gift that I can connect with them till the day I die.'

vii. Here is another story of creating a secure and confident childhood by supportive parents. **Sandhya Prakash**, Founder of Middle East Vegetarian Group (MEVEG) and CEO of Beacon Energy Systems, Dubai. Her company is a pioneer in recycling e-waste in UAE. She says, 'I was an all-rounder –class leader year on year and a leader on the sports field too. We lived in Narora, which is about 150 kilometers from Delhi. My father worked at the nuclear power plant. My parents never imposed any restrictions on us, my sister and I, we were never made to feel like we were girls. We cycled around fearlessly, took part in every activity we could. During that time, I happened to go to Mumbai to represent my school for a relay race. I was 14 then and what I saw of Mumbai convinced me that I wanted to take up a professional career. We went to Trombay for some races. That was the turning point. I realised that I had to get a good education to get to Mumbai. I studied hard, was a CBSE topper. BITS Pilani was the first institute to offer me a seat and I accepted readily.'

viii. **Vasanthi Hariprakash,** a journalist who has worked in print, TV and digital media, now based in Bengaluru says,

'I was impacted by Chitra Subramanian when she broke the Bofors scandal. I wrote a couple of essays mentioning that I wanted to be a journalist. It came instinctively to me to ask questions and get to the bottom of issues, though until then there were no journalists or media person in my family. Fortunately, my parents were encouraging of us sisters fulfilling our dreams.

'After I graduated in BSc Electronics, my desire was to get into the Indian Institute of Management (IIM) so, I took up the CAT exam, which I failed twice. That helped me finally realise that journalism is what I will love to pursue, not anything else. I got a kick out of my journalism course, which would not have happened with a management course or a corporate job. So I was doing things for the joy of it to the point where my passion met with my abilities. Your personality should be able to speak for your beliefs. Your confidence has to come through your body language.'

The confidence inculcated in these women by their families since childhood, stays with them throughout their lives, no matter what life throws at them. What happens in families where social compliance is built up, where women's careers are seen as a pre-marriage hobby?

A classic example would be my friend **Shagun** – she was brilliant in sport and had represented her country thrice in the Asian Games. She was nominated for the Arjuna award too but did not get it. The story needs to be repeated, for those who forget history are bound to repeat it... till it becomes a vicious circle.

Shagun's talent had blossomed under the encouragement of her coaches and parents. Driving her to catch the early morning train or bus to some godforsaken place wherever the training camp was being held, finding the money to pay for her expensive shoes and tickets were decisions her parents took because they believed in her talent. She went onto represent our country in many international championships and also the Asiad, held in India in 1982. But when the time came for her to convert her love for sport into a profession, parental approach changed. Shagun was prohibited from pursuing a sports career; because society had ordained that unmarried daughters with careers in sport bring shame to the family. They had, however, imposed the condition that she could play if her in-laws permitted it. Shagun, one of the fiercest women I have met, who used to brave Delhi's heat on an afternoon in May to make it to her basketball practice, however did not repeat history with her daughter's ambitions.

How can women open their mouths in a board room when as a girl she is taught to keep her mouth shut and let her family make all of her life's decisions?

Too often, lack of experience with arranging her own safety, women begin to take safety for granted and that somebody will 'protect' them or that most men are trustworthy.

On the other side of the coin, 'trustworthy' men may find that women, self-confident women, are a threat to their 'manhood' and they fall back on their default masculinity. Just like women fall back on the default feminine ways, when they get married.

As parents we assume our daughters will be protected by the men in their lives. That is a blind assumption we make. Because that makes the women careless about their own safety. Protection makes the protected weak, while safety is proactive and makes the person strong. Progressive

metropolitan residents may tend to dismiss family norms about women's safety as irrelevant or something which is required only in rural or semi urban pockets, they must not forget that:
- A large proportion of the entry point workforce are from smaller cities, towns and villages;
- At one point, they too grew up in a developing city, small town or village;
- They have been brought up by parents from smaller regions.

Seeds of social equality have to be planted – law alone cannot bring about affirmative changes in families, the revolution has to start within families, by evolving a more inclusive definition of patriarchy.

Interestingly, Baniya, Jain and Gujarati families have understood very well the evolving needs of a woman. Once the children have grown and daughters married off, the women often take up active roles in the family business, if they wish to. Many well-known women leaders in the present-day economy have evolved through this route, for example Meenakshi Saraogi, Chief Mentor of Balrampur Chini; Shobhana Bhartia, Chairperson and Editorial Director of *Hindustan Times* Group; Anu Aga, Director and ex Chairperson of Thermax Ltd; and Nita Ambani, Chairperson and founder of Reliance Foundation and non-executive Director of Reliance Industries.

But what happens to women who are married into families where a woman working is not a family-approved/prescribed norm?

Why do we provide our daughters 21st century resources – foreign education, travel, internships, standard of living –

then we weigh them down with century-old expectations. It's like using the engine of a Rolls Royce to pull a mule cart.

Victoria Beckham has loudly said, 'I want my kids to have a good work ethic. I believe you can achieve anything if you work hard enough to get it.' This builds self-reliance and a strong work ethic which ensures children's financial security. It will not remove bias, but teach them to overcome it, without sacrificing their jobs. This work ethic has defined the rise of capitalism.

There are some confidence-building interviews in the last chapter pulled out from my interviews with women who have managed to balance both – their personal identity and their professional identity.

CHAPTER 4

DECODING VENUS

THE QUEST OF an author is a driving need to answer a question – often personal. Till now I have been exploring the visible, physical manifestations of why women leave their workplace. However, the reasons are not always visible on the surface, or in the symptoms; rather, it bubbles in the layers just below the surface. The part where our beliefs reside.

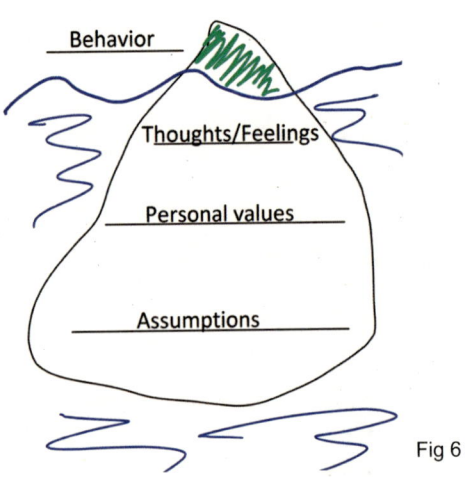

Fig 6

I explored ancient scriptures to explore further where these beliefs stem from.

In India, workplace is often called *karma bhoomi* (literally translated, it means a part of the earth where your actions are visible). I understand now that for women, perhaps their karma bhoomi is home + workplace and perhaps that is why their behaviour at their workplace is not separate from behaviour and intensity of emotion at home. Our feelings are not classified separately. That holds true for any gender. If a team leader refuses to give us leave for a situation at home or at workplace, the hurt is the same.

How each person expresses their hurt depends on their level of emotional maturity.

However, women's socialisation-growing up, makes them accountable for crises at home. When official permissions are required to discharge duties at home, these being non-negotiable, justify their dropping out from work.

So, up until a point we are cruising along based on our socialised roles. Suddenly, when men and women enter the workplace, both are thrown into the cauldron where they have to interact, with no experience on how to behave with the other gender, outside of family roles. We know ourselves and we assume socialisation norms will serve us here as well. So we start interacting based on random stereotypes that have been fed to us. It is here, navigating this interpersonal world that leadership emerges. Some get drowned in stereotypes, some learn to manipulate others in their quest for personal success. Only those who have a secure sense of self, can articulate their vision, and communicate based on a realistic understanding of each other, will come out as better persons, on the other side.

Emotional Intelligence (EI) is essential for us to survive in the work place, because we all work with people. Understanding our own biases and filters, moving beyond them, learning to identify other person's filters in order to not get overcome by it, are critical our personal growth.

Four pillars of Emotional Intelligence and Diversity which build these skills are:
- Knowing yourself,
- Social Architecting,
- Intercultural Literacy,
- Managing self.

While conducting such training, I find that, the real source of conflict and which has nothing to do with gender, is
a) The inability to express emotions – why I felt hurt / angry / disappointed / frustrated etc.
b) The inability to read those cues in others / understand if the other person needs comfort / knowledge / support / understanding / hug / listening.
c) The reluctance to ask for what I need – comfort / knowledge / support / understanding / hug / listening.

These emotional abilities / inabilities are 'standards of socially acceptable behaviour', structurally woven into the social fabric.

Some Dos and Don'ts are taught to us, while some come from our genetic make-up and sometimes, we learn. John Gray recognised it when he wrote *Men are from Mars & Women are from Venus*. Applying the same knowledge in a country like India in a patriarchal society will create havoc; because abroad the book was written with an intent for men to woo women. In India the same approach cannot be used to build teamwork in mixed teams.

I think the next stage of inclusion in a country that is largely patriarchal is going to come from:
   1. Building an inclusive society, which starts in school, home, college and reinforced at the workplace. Build

respect for other genders, explain behavioural dos and don'ts.
2. In school textbooks and the media, using gender imagery depicting women doing work in the kitchen and men wearing pants and going to the office needs to be stopped.
3. There must be emotional intelligence training at every level – school, college & workplace. The content will vary and keep the channel open for questions.

At a FICCI FLO gathering I attended, **Renuka Ramnath** ex MD & CEO of ICICI Ventures, was the chief guest. As head of the firm that she led, to reach the no. 1 position in the private equity space, it was surprising to hear that she left ICICI Ventures, as she faced the barrier of male clients unwilling to take financial advice from a woman. In 2010 she started her own firm, Multiples. Stereotypical beliefs in society may have prompted her to leave, but when it was her own firm, the barrier became just another incident in the day.

No wonder, that Multiples, her fund, now manages $1 billion of private equity funds in the span of seven years. The unspoken driver lay in her personal situation – a high need for autonomy, since she lost her husband in an accident. As her own boss, not only did she maximise her earning potential, but also created more autonomy to suit her family situation.

She understood that her client's inability was becoming her road block.

In a matrix with two goals – seeking autonomy vs money, we can develop a simple model to understand where women's drive takes them.

Imagine the deep level of understanding that an organisation has to build to harness diverse women power.

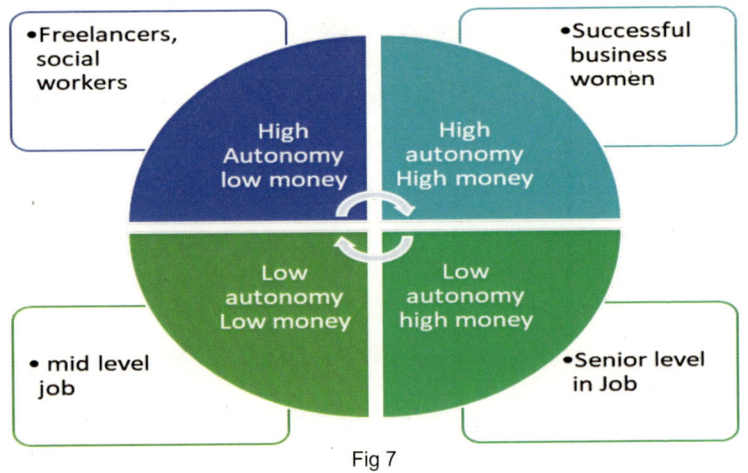

Fig 7

Maha-leadership – Integrated leadership

According to Hindu Vedic literature, Shiva or Mahadeva (Great God), embodies within Him attributes of all Mankind. Among the pantheon of Gods, Shiva is the Destroyer, while Brahma is the Creator and Vishnu the Preserver. The word Shiva is Anglicisation of the word Shav, which literally translated means inert body. In one of his avatars, Shiva is represented as Ardhnareeshwar, or half man, half woman.

My understanding of gender-based differences that I have internalised during the process of writing this book, shows me two things. One, that the road to reaching our potential lies in accepting the Self, beyond gender and beyond judgment. Two, the lives that we live, is based on gender stereotypes that have been fed to us since the moment we were born. Clothes that we wear, our outer selves are a product of the training given to perpetuate the stereotypes. Physiology decides what our gender is and our personality decides what its characteristics are. Everything else is a stereotypical belief.

The Ardhnareeshwar represents the fusion of characteristics of both genders, to become God-like. Shiva, thus, represents the channeling of one's power, which springs from an acute awareness of one's divinity, *not gender*; an intuitive awareness of the emotional nooks as much as the logical crannies.

Dr B N Raveesh, Forensic & Legal Psychiatrist at Mysore Medical College & Research Institute, has done extensive research on personality and its understanding based on ancient literature. In his book, *Ardhanareeshwara Concept: Brain and Psychiatry*, he says 'According to Hindu philosophy, among the 64 forms of Shiva, Ardhanareeshwara is a form, which means "the Lord that is half woman". In this form, Lord Shiva is seen as half man and half woman, with the left side being that of a woman'. Elsewhere he continues, 'This fusion of Shiva and Shakti representing the male and female halves transcends the distinction between and limitation of male and female. It takes the Lord to the level of beyond-gender, manifest(ing) Brahman'. *Brahman* is a Sanskrit word, which literally means 'ultimate realisation'.

When we look at Shiva from this perspective – where the feminine co-exists with the masculine in all humans – we will find that not all skills, capabilities, arts, professions, and creativity are gender specific. How much of it we bring into play, or throttle in the myriad roles we play in our lives is what matters. Masculine and feminine are mere associations of the form that we choose to display. Moreover, by attaching it to gender labels, we limit others and our capabilities. By putting labels, we draw attention to some characteristics, which reveals our own limited thinking.

Zero Bias Boards

It would be erroneous to assume that 'all' men are analytical or feel threatened, while 'all' women are emotional or subdued. It cannot be generalised – some men are confident about bringing forth their emotional side, while some women are more confident, expressing their analytical side. We have merely created these labels based on what we know, conditioning, societal pressure and stereotypes. Men too have emotions, but society and families frown upon men expressing their feelings. Similarly, women may be extremely logical, but society rejects that by labeling the behaviour as bossy, hyper or callous. This is social / behavioural conditioning, exactly similar to Pavlov's experiment. Only difference is that instead of electric shocks, we use peer group pressure.

What comes in our way are our deep-level values about gender, which have formed part of our belief system. *This needs to be updated, based on a realistic assessment.* Handling leadership situations, therefore, appears to revolve more on individual perception of a situation and reconditioning ourselves based on true understanding.

One particular mannerism of my husband continued to irritate me for many years. Every time I would drop something on the kitchen floor or platform while cooking, he would rush in with a paper towel to wipe it clean. He would scrub, scrub… off the damn spot. There was no getting away from this habit of his. Till one day, I changed my filter. Instead of the perspective of the perfect cook wanting total autonomy in the kitchen, I changed my perspective to really 'see' him as a husband not bound by stereotypes, wanting to keep the kitchen clean. My reaction changed from anger to pointing out other spots which needed cleaning. I revised my myth – that the kitchen is a woman's domain. Frankly it was such a relief, by letting go of one irrelevant belief, I freed myself from so much anguish.

We all wear filters – multiple ones, in fact. Some arising from our past experience, personality, culture, gender, knowledge, profession, ethnic group, religion. Within filters there can be sub-filters. These filters determine how we interpret a situation, respond to it and communicate our response or screw up our relationships.

Filters are clearly evident in behaviour, and behaviour has consequences. A closer look at beliefs will reveal that filters have emotions associated with them, either happy ones or otherwise.

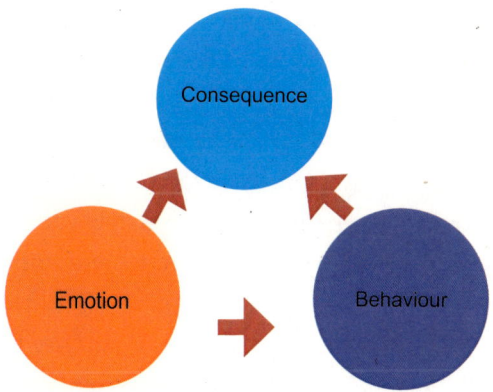

Fig 8 Taken from Askgeet's Emotional Intelligence and Diversity Training workshop

Socialisation is a cultural divide created in society and that is where it has to be addressed. The 4 – 7% women on the boards who rise through sheer talent, are unaware of any barriers.

Studies show that adolescent girls in schools, who were exposed to successful female role models in their everyday environment, are much more adventurous in their career choices. This fact is corroborated by the interviews. In each one, wherever parents have had high expectations from their daughters, free of stereotypical choices, the women have been led by what they wanted to pursue as opposed to what their parents, in-laws or society wants them to.

A word which came up very frequently during my conversations was the word 'my mom', indicating the importance of the nurturer in developing the seeds of self-esteem and identity. This word represented for women either a life they wanted to follow or avoid, depending upon their experience of it. The influences were often vocal and sometimes subtle. Seeds of an unshakeable sense of self-worth are laid during childhood. Even mentoring by the first boss cannot lay as strong a foundation as a secure and confident childhood.

Socialisation teaches women to adopt characteristics from role models of their gender. By default, the role models they have been exposed to, are mostly submissive women – the one who 'adjusts'. Brought up in a protective environment, they may be good at listening, caring, eager to learn, meek, averse to risks. This became evident from the words used to describe moms/female role models – empathetic, democratic, common sense, supportive, well read, knowledgeable, articulate or good listener. Other words like 'duty' also came up. Even dressing sense and general mannerisms was referred to as 'not to invite attention', or provoke men.

In contrast, the words used to describe dads/male role models were – authoritative, bossy, trustworthy, risk taker, have a separate identity, courage, visionary and task master. Even words like 'taking people along' or 'guide' were used in connection with work done in the office, thus synonymous with male behaviour.

Perhaps gender connection with the mother sees women adopting their mother's qualities (fair, honest, reasonable and being empathetic) as behavioural dictionary. When men see women adopting male traits, they mentally reject them as bosses. This socialisation imbalance is a critical part of unlearning in the road to accepting women as leaders.

Here I quote Sudhir Kakar from his book, *The Inner World*, to emphasise the point, 'The adult personality of Indian women is not only molded through this (unconscious) manipulation of her precarious feelings of worthiness as an adolescent, it is also distinctly influenced by the culturally-sanctioned maternal indulgence of daughters. Daughterhood in India is not without its rewards, precisely because the conditions of womanhood are normally so forbidding'.

Another excerpt reads, 'Women do not sentimentalise their mothers in this way (as compared with sons). For daughters, the mother is not an adoring figure on a pedestal; she is a more earthy presence, not always benign but always there'.

This book is my way of telling women that devaluation is only a short-term solution. In the long-term, stunted trees only produce more stunted trees. I know the picture is not pretty. But it is the truth. Our culture is about Constance, while today the world is about flux. Therefore, each of us has to find our equilibrium, based on our reality and choices, be it Venus or Mars.

CHAPTER 5

A LEVEL PLAYING FIELD

I FOUND THE most comprehensive list of laws pertaining to Women, in force today, on https://testbook.com/static-gk/laws-protecting-women-in-india

The Protection of Women from Domestic Violence Act	2005
The Dowry Prohibition Act	1961
The Sexual Harassment of Women at Workplace (Prevention, Prohibition and Redressal) Act	2013
The Medical Termination of Pregnancy Act	1971
The Maternity Benefit Act	1961
The Equal Remuneration Act	1976
The Prohibition of Child Marriage Act	2006
The Hindu Succession Act	1956
The Indecent Representation of Women (Prohibition) Act	1986
The National Commission for Women Act	1990

Most of these laws flow from women's social roles arising out of Marriage. Let us face it, it is the single most defining change in a women's life. In every person's life there are three phases – Birth, Puberty and Death. But in a woman's life there are five – birth, puberty, marriage, child bearing and death.

How marriage and child bearing are forever going to

impinge on a woman's freedom, nobody tells her. But that discussion is for another day. What I am wondering is that – today women are running corporations generating thousands of crores of revenue, even then do they require other laws to ensure they can function in a free and fearless way? Just think about it for a minute then continue reading. This role arises out of her gender, over which she has no control.

At work a different reality exists – where also she is now present; where it is not her gender which comes into play, but her knowledge, talent, capability and thinking. But because the systems have been run by men for men, the rules of the game will have to change for the working women. At least, that is what a working woman in India is expected to do at the workplace. The woman has to conform to man-made rules, the rules at workplaces are not adjusted to a woman's needs and what women are taught. What they are taught are also not changed to suit workplace culture in India.

I Equal Opportunity for Jobs

Lacunas exist due to evaluation criteria being set around male qualities – strength, height, voice, ability to travel etc.

We have discussed enough in previous chapters the problems arising from **Social Structure**. These norms translate into a financial loss for the women, as depicted in the fig. A society that takes away her chance of her becoming financially independent, and gives her nothing in return. Today most women are not assured of share in either husband's nor father's property. While a guy has the opportunity to work and earn as well as is entitled to father's property. As parents and lawmakers we have to think about the fairness of it.

At mid-career level, they are denied of their economic right to continue with their jobs by:

EQUAL OPPORTUNITY FOR JOBS

- All entry level require late night shifts, Maket covering, field visits.

- At entry level, it matteres how much time & initiative fresher is taking in learning, completing tasks.

- Hindered by parental and in-laws attitude to jobs, travelling, sitting late.

- At mid career level she is not likely to get job employer comes to know that she is married, or planning to start a family Or has in-laws tha will need taking care of

1) Laying her off when organisation comes to know a woman is pregnant.
2) Make her sit in the office till late at night just to satisfy some ego need of the boss, or call her on her day off. These are tactics designed so that women will resign on their own.
3) Deducting money for coming late and not paying her overtime. Some companies have started converting leaves into money and deduct that from your salary if you take leave plus also deduct leave from your entitlement.
4) In many companies, women will be given minimal increment, because employer knows that she will neither fight for increment nor will she leave.

These are systemic issues which can be corrected by the government's well laid out inspection machinery. It is just that the parameters related to women working also need to be separately scrutinised. Women need to have the assurance that the government is there for them, ensuring an equal opportunity space.

There can be a mandatory health checkup for women once she is pregnant. In fact her job should be protected till her maternity period leave is over, or she is in a position to find another job. This rule can apply irrespective of whether it is a corporate, NGO, MSE or MSME.

I have seen in many organisations where there is a robust women's group, women come forward to solve their problems on their own. Every organisation must have a women's association which will function under the aegis of HR Departments. All issues of workplace harassment, bullying, unfair discrimination have to be brought to the notice of the association, before being taken to HR. This will ensure that the victim's name is not publicised, nor victimised. Only name of person who bullies, discriminates in publicised and HR Dept has to demonstrate action. Report of association's activities can also be signed off by Inspector. This will ensure that HR is accountable to the women for redressal and not to the CEO. Like Exit Analysis, these reports also have to be mandatorily shared in Balance Sheet so that public knows the actual risks due to untoward behavior of male bosses.

This group can randomly interview some of the women candidates attending interviews, to check if such candidates are being asked sexist questions like what does your husband do? Who will look after your parents / children in your absence? Etc. etc.

In fact, just like POSH, there should be mandatory training of men on how to interview women where she is not denied of her economic right due to her gender. It can be called **Prevention of Unfair Rejection (POUR)**.

The most unfair wrong which is happening in front of our eyes is that when every organisation knows that 50% of the women are going to drop out before they reach department head level, then why is it that organisations are not monitoring this figure? Diversity and Inclusion is just not about hiring marginalised segments, it's also about retaining those segments. If organisations are measured on their ability to retain people, then retaining women is a metric which has to be monitored separately, as it spells that things are 'right' with the organisation.

I am not forgetting that in India there two types of women in the workforce, for which Policymakers monitor measures separately –

1) Women in rural areas form the bulk of unorganised labour. These women may be illiterate or may have very basic education. Women in rural India have a different set of issues. This fact became evident to me When Zelma Lazarus said, 'Girls get married at the age of 13 & 14 and start producing babies soon enough. Government gives them special rations, but they never get it. Because we are working with the government, we have requested the government to give us the ration so that we can give it to them. ISKCON cooks it for us. The other day, one of these little girls, I was watching her, she looked half dead, she had hardly a bump. So I asked her how many months she was, she said 7 months, no bump. I asked her, do you eat the food we are giving? She said that her husband will beat her if she doesn't bring the food home. 'I put it in a bag and hide it in my saree and take it home.' I quietly told an assistant from the village to go to the husband and talk to him, that the girl will not live through the pregnancy. So the husband says, 'we are 4 brothers. I don't know who the father is'. That's the state of affairs, two hours out of Mumbai'.

2) Educated women in urban areas who form part of the organised labour force. These women have skills which are marketable.

We have to understand that the problems assailing these women are different and so are the solutions.

My research has mainly covered the second category. I believe that improvement in either one will have impact on the other as well. If access to health and education is improved for women in first category, their aspirations will increase, as Gursharan mentions in her interview, motivating them to increase their skills and try for skilled jobs. Various interview shared in this book demonstrate the truth in my words. That is why any investment in women's initiative, has an impact on the community.

In the second category falls the leaking pipeline problem, which is a great visual for focusing women-centric initiatives.

This is but one strong evidence of how social norms work have hitherto worked in favour of men, to keep financial

control of companies in the hands of men. It is a ground reality which needs a grounded solution. When women realise that the social system has conspired to deny them economic opportunity, they find practical ways to solve the problem.

The role of women or rather her 'job description (JD)' has also differed with religion and geography. For instance, Hindu women in South follow different set of customs while women in Bihar follow different ones. To these differences, add the job description of a company, the nuances of an NGO, MNC, SME, Public company etc. etc. These multiple complications, – no HR System is designed around these differences nor are HR Managers trained to handle them. Cultural sensitivity / Gender Sensitivity training can correct this abnormality. It is the nation's agenda, not at the company's discretion.

This Cultural / Gender Sensitivity training can fulfil dual purpose. A) Through group work, like walking in each other's shoes, men can be sensitized to issues women face in their presence. B) Through Case Study and In-Basket exercises, women can be trained to realign their priorities, gear themselves up to fulfil organizational and leadership requirements and iron out the geographical / religious nuances.

My personal view is that since it is always more laborious to rewrite the old, and Corporates already have the infrastructure to train people during induction, it would make sense to train new comers on these nuances.

We have to create the right environment so that she has **Equal Opportunity to Career Growth.**

For far too long, gender and sex has been very narrowly defined. *It is time to remove gender labels from 'work' so that we can accept each other's strengths and limitations and learn to work together as cohesive teams.*

This has come through a process of introspection and

processing my emotion in an environment where expression of emotions is 'trainer-led'. That is where 'enlightenment' can be initiated.

All that law can do is 'protect', but encouragement has to come from need of the hour.

CHAPTER 6

STRATEGIC IMPLICATIONS FOR WOMEN'S CAREER

ABRAHAM MASLOW'S THEORY, *The Hierarchy of Needs*, has provided an overall structure to understand human needs. As a psychologist who studied motivation levels of people in organisations, he established a hierarchy of needs which drives people. Initially he had identified 5 needs – physiological, safety, affiliation, esteem and self-actualisation. Over the years, three more were added – cognitive, aesthetic and transcendence.

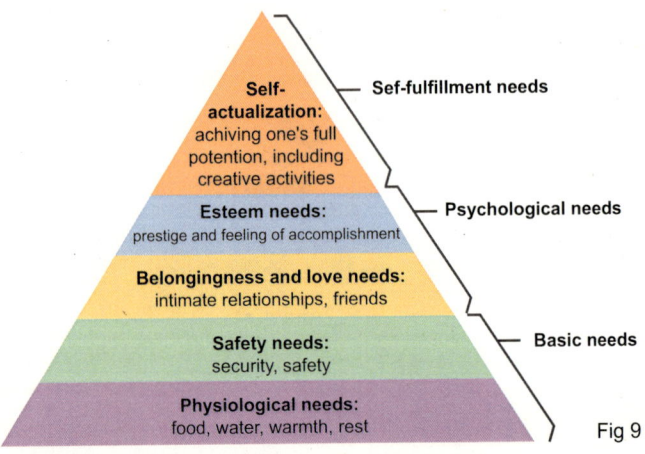

Fig 9

As a human resource professional, my first instinct is to point out how these needs change for women as they transition through their life stages. If we were to break down a woman's career into two broad trends, we will find two distinct reasons why women leave the work place:

Stage 1 - 28 to 32 age group where family attitudes/support was the critical differentiator. In case of single women, not many major breaks were seen.

Stage 2 - 42 to 45 age group where lack of satisfaction/opportunity for expressing their talent was the differentiator.

At the beginning of their careers, women's motivation needs may be similar to that of men, because they want the same things as men – money, good designation and career growth. But with the birth of a child, the child's basic needs become more important. At this stage her objective is not to compete, but to supplement the family income and keep her dreams alive. If leaving is dictated by social constraints, then supplementary support can keep her in the system. Mentoring at this stage should not be only work-related, but also about how to handle concerns, objections at home and financial stability.

Since confidence building at home has had the maximum effect on the longevity of a women's career, perhaps it is time that external support be strengthened to serve the company's objective of retaining women. After all, they too want all the comforts that financial success brings. As Sonika Iqbal suggests, 'Planners can help empower women if they remember that she has a dual role to play, and build that into whatever plans they have for them. Circumstances surrounding women prevent them from taking up opportunities and climbing the corporate ladder in spite of their education, training and experience'.

With age and maturity, once safety, esteem and self-actualisation needs have been satisfied, cognitive, aesthetic and transcendence needs become more prominent, which may or may not be dissimilar to men. However, what are the factors which prevent senior management teams from assigning projects to women which utilise their experience, is a matter which requires further study within each organisation. These factors could be personal limitations or assumptions which stem from a patriarchal history of organisation's culture. It would be erroneous to believe otherwise. These assumptions need to be tested against facts, on a self-awareness framework and group dynamics that is the first premise of Emotional Intelligence.

If we were to examine Fig 2 again, we will find:
1. Context of patriarchy governs attitudes towards women's education, health, employment and representation in parliament. While,
2. Demand and supply of labour determines Wages, which is an economic reality.

The former skews the latter though the answer lies in better awareness of the latter.

Today I see most women starting their own businesses, to render value based on what they have to contribute. The economic accelerator seems to be to provide them skill, education and finance.

Turn to the later chapter to read a case study based on how **Sally Holkar**'s work with the weaving community of Maheshwar, changed the society as a whole, when women took up weaving. How people collaborate and form teams when they have a common goal and are available in one place. This would be the perfect example of a self-managed team where, I am sure, one will never hear complaints about leaving on time because the community is working for the family's benefit.

A study by Sylvia Ann Hewlett, Chairman and CEO of the Centre for Talent Innovation (CTI), an NGO based in New York, points to how India can show the way, on leveraging talent across the divides of gender, generation, geography, and culture. According to Sylvia, while women all around the world face a barrage of barriers – both cultural and professional, at home and the workplace – blocking their ability to pick up their careers where they left, Indian women have succeeded in on-ramping. This has been made possible not only due to the growth of the Indian market but also because of the relative age of women; as the pipeline of experienced talent is simply not large enough to ignore this pool of professionally-qualified women.

Her research also highlighted that 72% of women, who want to take up their careers from where they left off, do not want to return to the same company they left. Dissatisfaction with their rate of career progression drives almost as many women out of the workforce, as absence of good childcare facilities.

Work places need to be aligned with women's nature – what drives them, their body cycles, their priorities and rules which work well with their family life. That is why we see so many women converting their hobbies into businesses. If that is what will take for women to find work which is aligned with their nature, then let us give them business education along with their professional courses. They can start something of their own after a few years of work experience. Work becomes a place of worship when it is an expression of the self rather than a place of sacrificing oneself.

Worlds today exist on economies. Finland, where women's

issues are taking center stage now because of increasing political representation of women in parliament, has a lady Prime Minister, one among many other countries. The No. 1 country globally on World Economic Forum's Global Gender Equality ranking, has always been among the Top Three on the rankings for many years now, because of the culture of equal opportunity. The top country with the least gender gap and most equality in 2023 is Iceland. The global Top Five is completed by three other Nordic countries – Norway (87.9%, 2nd), Finland (86.3%, 3rd) and Sweden (81.5%, 5th) – and one country from East Asia and the Pacific – New Zealand (85.6%, 4th). Countries gain when equal opportunity is the mantra.***

You might say, India was the first country to have a woman prime minister, Madame Indira Gandhi, still women are not empowered. Agreed. Indira Gandhi was very intuitive and decisive and intelligent. She didn't need anybody's permission to empower herself. She was involved in politics from childhood, it was in her blood; she was a parliamentarian. It came with the territory – being Nehru's daughter and in the center of the political cauldron.

Similarly other woman also grow up in their family profession's / business cauldron. It takes whatever it takes. You are empowered if you feels so.

At present, in India around 15% of the total members of the 17th Lok Sabha (2019-2024) are women while in State legislative assemblies, women on average constitute 9% of the total members. This is a reflection of women's involvement

---

*** https://www.weforum.org/publications/global-gender-gap-report-2023/in-full/benchmarking-gender-gaps-2023/

in national affairs. The moment the reality changes, women controlling more and more of businesses, professions, when they start carrying more than 50% of the economic clout, the figures will be reflected in parliament too.

Building a Transcendent Leadership

Prachi Rastogi says, '...from a very young age, I always knew what I didn't want – no mathematics, no marketing. I wanted a profession which involved interacting with people. I didn't want to go out of Delhi as I am deeply interested in spirituality and have adopted that as a life choice. The ashram I have adopted has centers in Delhi.

'I don't want to live my life based on money and mundane values. For me, life has a meaning which goes beyond the usual consumerism. I have lived in an OSHO ashram since I was 17. My spiritual master helps me in my inner and outer journey. I have not come into this world to earn money. You see people are the same, creative across organisations and emotions. Where does it go? That energy ultimately goes into destruction, power plays. Work becomes the end. I am inculcating healthy living in the office, helping leaders walk the talk.'

Women channelise resources for betterment of societies, communities and families. I watched Indra Nooyi on YouTube, trying to decode her brand of leadership as she spoke about health issues that America faces and how Pepsi re-aligned their product portfolio to focus on pursuing health and wellness. In the same breath, she touched upon issues being faced by a career-oriented woman in running a household. She sounded like any Indian mother telling her child to finish her food.

In this scenario, where We, the Women of India have a lot

going for us:
- The right to vote
- Education
- Family structure
- Domestic support
- Women are worshipped vs treated as commodity
- A growing economy
- Many unexplored professions

We should seize the day, help other women and continue with our jobs, career, businesses, because if we stop, we become the bottle necks.

If norms around family and marriage have to evolve, then law can play a part there.

I have talked about women operating in their social roles and of the economic opportunities they need to seize. I am waiting to see the New Indian Woman emerge when she is operating NOT from her gender, nor from economic compulsion, but from her **potential**.

It is high time the world gets to see what Indian women are capable of achieving.

CHAPTER 7
DISCOVERY

I. Methodology:

As an HR professional, I was keen on sensing 'the heart of the matter' i.e. the social, psychological, emotional, economic factors at the core of the issue.

Therefore, I got in touch with women randomly, in my networks. Many of them opened their hearts and their lives to share with me the real world of where they work, their *karmabhoomi* (field of action).

I contacted about 70 to 80 women over a period. Only criterion I used was that they should have taken a career break at some point or another and that they represented a cross section of geography and function. An online survey captured some details to understand the demographic similarities and differences in the sample group. Just 56 interviews materialised – over skype, some face to face and some on phone.

Here is a list of the questions:

1. What are the key challenges faced in pursuit of your career? How did you overcome them? Did you require any extra support and from whom to face that challenge?
2. Who and what influenced your Leadership Style as a Role Model?

3. What were the key factors responsible for your growth?
4. Did you face any kind of biases/pre- conceived notions/ resentment from male/female colleagues/ difference in the way male & female subordinates and colleagues respond to your leadership? How did you handle that?
5. How do you renew yourself? How much time do you spend on it and self-learning and growth?
6. What measures can be adopted to have more women in corporate board rooms – in your opinion?
7. Could the organisation have done something to support the transition?
8. How much time do you spend on your own learning? And what activities you undertake?

I did not use all the interviews, as many of the respondents chose to give non-committal answers. One interview did not get recorded properly.

The interviews were analysed to identify the burning issues and commonalities and differences, to understand:

Reasons women leave the workplace,

Issues they face,

Factors responsible for their rise up the career and leadership ladder.

These are recorded interviews, a qualitative impression of their leadership journey. I chose the qualitative route as I found that while there are many quantitative studies available, there were not very many qualitative accounts of what women 'feel' when they encounter gender bias at the workplace; as emotional reactions drive actions and behaviour and especially of women which determine behavior in economic society per se.

Behaviour matters!

Secondly, for my sample, I decided to interview a mix of

women well healed in leadership as well as women new to leadership, to capture issues and insights at each stage. Most of the respondents are women who started out in managerial positions and became leaders as part of their natural career progression.

Data from 46 of the interviews was used to arrive at the findings.

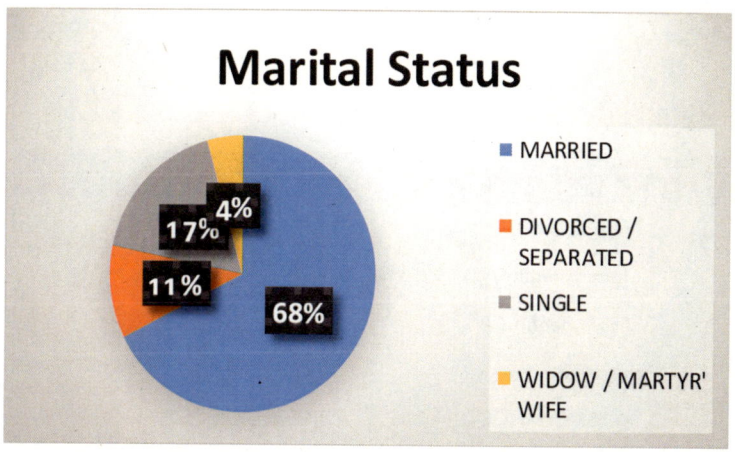

Academics

Qualifications	Nos
M Phil	1
Post Graduates	22
Ph Ds	4
Technical degree	6
Graduates	13

Reason for leaving	Nos
bullying	2
family health	4
own health	3
spouse relocation	4
CAREER CHANGE	3
Marriage	1
entrepreneur	1
unsupportive family	1
Retired	1
study leave	3

III. Other Random Observations noted:
- With women, authenticity counts.
- Expectations from girls are huge differentiators.
- As leaders, in the absence of any leadership model that they can refer to, women tend to use values learnt at home – fair, honest, reasonable and being empathetic, as compasses. Women need to invest in educating themselves on leadership style.
- Mostly in subservient jobs because job- related training focuses on 'mould'ing their behaviour.
- Women are hesitant about using their own strengths in their leadership capacity – probably because they are fearful of being rejected as leaders by their male followers and bosses.
- Women lack self-confidence as leaders. There is a constant need to seek approval from bosses, colleagues – mostly male.
- Late night meetings and client sit visits are the breaking point. The tussle between domestic burden and raising kids is on the women. They are constantly running away from challenges because of the domestic burden.
- Women need to talk about the problems – be ashamed of ignoring them.
- Cultural inhibitions are all in the head – doesn't matter to the client. What matters is results. Client wants credible information. All the wining and the dining are the extras.
- Men want a team leader who tells them exactly what is required to be done, they like structure, like the rules of a game.
- Women drop out due to lack of support systems because they hesitate to invest in a support structure or fail to have goals. They are keener to indulge in their personal

interests rather than arrange their lives around their career – reinforced behaviour.
→ Have to be really selfish – organisation exists as an environment – put your own milestones first. It's for you to figure out what you want – that's the magnet.
→ I don't think it is about gender as it is about being effective or not effective – at a task.
→ Stop whining for a good supportive boss OR support from higher ups.
→ Women need to be trained on pitching their voice to make themselves heard.
→ Women tended to see only two challenges – home and work. Those who saw a challenge in the macro environment, stayed.

II. Capability Building interviews
Aishwarya Joshi
Changing career even when you are doing well

> *Current Position: a certified CSR practitioner, who has evolved as an architect for humanity. She holds diverse roles in the United Nations' local projects, is part of the Health Authority – Abu Dhabi Campaign and a finalist for Dubai for Acumen's social enterprise competition.*

Aishwarya, an architect with a passion for building sustainable community and planet, started her career as an architect in Dubai. After proving herself, 'I took up CSR of my own accord – it was self-motivated. The possibility of independence, freedom of thought, taking responsibility in the correct direction to bring about social change, communicating ideas and thoughts at the right time to get the right results etc. was what attracted me to the job. I didn't want a big salary. Thankfully I have enjoyed the life I wanted; I have been able to blur the line between work and play.

'I lost my parents when I was 16 and my perspective and needs are defined because of the journey that I took alone. I became self-reliant at a very young age. My career as a lead consultant in architecture was lucrative. Unlike kids of my age, I had developed the habit of saving at an early age, which is now helping me make good career choices. In my profession, decisions are made based on understanding of one culture, adapting them. Sometimes getting the same results can be a challenge; therefore, if a change in strategy can create the same impact, then it's just about how you decide to go around the mountain.

'Speaking of gender roles, I have found men are more available for the job. However, I have never experienced a conflict or hindrance, if you are open, people are open to sharing their resources. It's all about communication and integrity. I have met some extremely intelligent and supportive local people (Dubai). There is a hesitation only at the beginning. I have never given instructions. I suggest in a way that is doable for my team member. There is ownership for the projects they handle. I believe that I am not here to create followers but more leaders.'

Jeroze Dalal
Aspiring to be MD

Current Position: Strategic Business Unit Head, Novartis

'I find very few women in senior top management positions, in almost all organisations I have worked with. Today, organizations encourage recruiting women at all levels, but one still finds the top-level positions dominated by men. I have come across some women professionals who have chosen their career over marriage.

'There are male colleagues who can be strong competitors. Their strength lies in the fact that they are connected all day and are available to global colleagues sitting in different continents. For me, I have to demarcate my work and home life. When I'm at home, I want to do justice on that front, unless there are some burning issues that may need to be urgently addressed. Work to me is a subset of my life, not life itself. I also had the opportunity to work with a team in Pakistan, Singapore, Thailand and Philippines and South Africa and I have not found any difference in the way they respond to my leadership.

'I have always been fascinated to be a Managing Director of a company – it could be the MD of a clinical research company or better still, an NGO working in healthcare sector. What I like about this is having a holistic view of the business and driving it in a manner that truly makes a difference in the lives of people. Not that I will do anything for it. If it doesn't happen, it doesn't happen. As long as I am aiming to reach there, I am happy.

'One day, I hope my family, particularly my children, will be proud of me. I have tried very hard to multi-task, balance my home and work life and to be there for the family whenever required –although I may not have been there physically when they returned from school. I explained to them that mummy has a responsible job, a demanding one that requires a lot of thinking, planning and I wouldn't be able to take some days off unless I have planned in advance; I also have to ensure that nobody is inconvenienced. Even if I am sick and unable to reschedule all my appointments, I still make it to work. I try to set the right example.

'Working for almost three decades has not been a bed of roses. Like my research guide used to say, 'Jahannum mein jaane ke liye, marna padtaa hain' (if you want to go to hell, you must first be prepared to die). But with all the efforts invested, I also take time to enjoy – I have travelled to many countries, pursued my interests and made few but very good friends. I have soaring ambitions but am equally value-driven. I will follow my heart and do what I think is right without asking for any favors. On a positive note, I shall end by saying with my clean conscience, conscientious and diligent style and a fantastic can-do attitude, I will survive!

'One of the challenges was when I began travelling for work. I was very scared to tell at home that I will be going to Lucknow, Varanasi and Ghaziabad. My family asked me why I was being sent. I tried to answer very diplomatically – probably the sales team in these locations is less knowledgeable and may not ask many difficult questions. It was the first time that I was asked to travel. And the first time itself, I faced every kind of conceivable problem – cancelled flights and the seven-day trip got extended to 11 days as these places were only accessible by overnight train journeys. I survived. Once I reached there, I was taken very good care of. The group was completely male dominated; medical reps are generally all guys. They were very respectful but I am sure they must have wondered whether a woman can teach them anything new. The right attitude – modesty, willingness to learn from their experience and a little cool and balanced mindset, helped. I tailored my presentation for the audience, involved the team members and acknowledged their inputs (after all they have worked in the field for 25 years, while I was standing there with barely a year's experience). It may take time for male colleagues to accept you as their supervisor. But once done, you have to keep inspiring them, and raise the bar each time.'

Meenal Bhat
How to lead a team

Current Position: Now Founder - Kraftland Consults for 12 years+

After doing her civil engineering and an MBA from the Asian Institute of Management, she started her career with Johnson & Johnson. However, a shift in her priorities after the birth of her second child, brought her back to Gurgaon as the boss of her own company. Today she employs eight other people.

'From my mom I learnt patience…patience…patience… Can you imagine as kids we have never ever been slapped, and hardly scolded at? Her idea of disciplining was, "I will speak to you when you are in a better mood." And no, "I will not allow you to do something that I think is wrong". And I have the world's best mom-in-law. Again, she has the patience. She quit her job once we had a baby… said that she has already sacrificed her career for her kids, so it's better if she quits.

'If one has to change oneself to fit in that's where rifts happen. The ideology is simple – I have these buckets, things I am okay with to give up, things that are just too much me and I care too much about it to give up. So things that I am okay with, I don't even bother to negotiate on. My mom-in-law is the boss of the house; she takes my opinion but she is the boss.

'My leadership style is similar to my dad's, though our industries are completely different. I never realised I was using his style till a person in my team gave me that feedback.

'In the knowledge industry, since it's all about generating reports – the norm is that a manager gives the team everything that has to be done – and checks on them. Assumption is, analyst does not know what needs to be done – I do things the other way round. My ideology is that since the analyst is spending so much time researching the subject, they are the experts. So as soon as the project starts, I would explain the client's business objective and divide the work into pieces that fulfill that objective; each person, no matter how low in hierarchy, is responsible for the piece and in that sense becomes an expert and they take complete responsibility of their pieces. My job, instead of checking whether it is right or not, was to ask questions about how the objective was addressed and not whether they have made mistakes. My boss initially thought I was mad! But I was super lucky. I had the best performing project team.

'Even people who don't have great outputs would become so involved in work that it was a wonderful sight. I was convinced I was given the best team; but then I started getting people who were not considered as good. And even they delivered. As a matter of fact, HR told me one day that I was the only manager who had no issues with people's deliverables. Over the past six years I would have delivered more than 150 projects, messed up just one.

'The other thing which I think I have is the ability to own up for my team; anything that goes right is individually celebrated while when it goes wrong, it is my mistake because I was managing the show.

'If you ask my team, the strings are held so lightly yet tightly that they don't think there is someone guiding them. It was just them delivering. As I said, I completely take a back seat. There is trust that the outputs have been well researched and if things need to go back, come out in those discussions, before reports are sent out. The responsibility to answer the question lies with the analyst.

'The thing is, I have never seen the world as different for men and women so I may not answer this well. This style can be and has been an issue for people who like control – I don't see it as a men and women thing but a personality thing. I was lucky my boss would manage the boss and let me do things my way… hoping the project doesn't fail!

'About industry-specific prejudices, I can talk about two segments within the same industry – one was on the product side – there were not many women leaders anyway – but though the management wanted to bring in more women, the challenge was – we got picked up from the campuses at a level much higher than existing people, so that increased the conflict, given that you are a woman!

'I had this incident that a very important customer asked me out! I didn't know how to handle it! This was my first month in the job. Had the company asked me to work with him, I would have quit. But it didn't even come to that. When I told the head, thankfully he just said come back, no need to work in that territory.

'Professionally, the challenge came when I moved from an MNC to an unknown company as we needed to move to Delhi after our first child. I was also traveling too much and though given a transfer, the travel would have continued, else I would have to take more of a support role which also I was not comfortable with, so I decided to move to a desk job in a smaller company; still not back end. I loved my job at my previous company, I was growing fast, was learning a lot; being under the fast track programme, I knew the leadership team across APAC. To leave all of that and move to a desk job was a BIG decision.

'I gave up work because I was always tired. For about a year I was working part time; first as a consultant with my own company and then started picking up projects from outside. I have my own company now. This year it moved from being a single person company to a more formal structure and people on rolls. I am working full time now, in my company.

'However, each of these events has wonderfully shaped my life the way it is today. Having worked and known so many people in my first company, plus the consulting experience from my second company has helped me with my work. In these two years since I started, I have not asked anyone for projects. Clients come themselves to see if I am available.

'I find Indian women or at least the ones I have seen, tend to be more emotionally involved. But I see this true of Asia, high emotional involvement. I have also worked with women leaders across 14 countries in Asia, all the same. Australia is different. What is good about the Western system is that work and home is slotted. Here it's a part of life. I don't know what's good or bad, but just different.

'I have learnt a few things from a friend regarding utilising woman power. He hires women – married with kids/responsibilities at home, so they need flexi hours. He has been able to target a pool of highly-educated women who just for the need of flexibility are not working; these are engineers who otherwise would be housewives! Another thing is safety. While in MNCs even your boss could not ask you to stay back after 6 pm; though car was provided to everyone, if you did stay back the boss had to make sure you reached home safely.'

Nandini Goswami
How to be fearless

> *Current Position: Head of Corporate Communications for an MNC in India, Nandini started her career as a journalist with The Hindustan Times. She has worked in different aspects of the Communications business - Reputation and issues management, media management, business & internal communications and CSR.*

'A lot of investment is made through talking and engaging with team which I learnt from my mom, a journalist. She has retired now…she is 74. She was with the BBC radio those days. I learnt while observing her, the way she dealt with people and most important, how she managed me. She had tremendous clarity of thought, extremely determined. Maa's negotiation skills were fantastic; very strong woman… she worked at the time when journalism was a male-dominated area. I have seen her beautifully manage situations.

'So far, I haven't seen any difference in the way my team responds to me. I also feel that is because I see myself as a manager – not a man or woman, and treat them the same. I have always been open to feedback. If their response has been negative, I expect a reason from them. In a work place, we are the same.

'While women have their own set of personal responsibilities, I think it is important to strike a balance at work. I am saying this because I am a single working mom and my son is fifteen. There are times my work does get demanding with travel etc. I don't step back because I am a woman. I work extra hard, to make sure neither fronts suffer. On a lighter note it does take a toll on me. But the reward of having overcome is fantastic.

'I would say, as a value what women lag behind in is calling a spade a spade. I feel in India different parts of the country have a different attitude towards women. The least discriminatory, I would say is Mumbai, culturally it is an extremely professional place. Having said that, when you come across someone from another part of the country where women are not expected to be firm, men may find it difficult to handle strong women.

'I also feel that that there should be more women at a senior level in marketing and sales. I think a lot of them tend to take breaks during child birth and go a little slow then. I also feel many women who have a family, feel they have something to fall back upon.

'Networking has helped me a lot – learning from other people's experiences – meeting senior leaders, who sometimes champion you, it happens.'

Neela Satyanarayan
On being the first Lady in Maharashtra IAS Cadre

In the later years of her life, Neela Satyanarayan spent her time writing books, songs, screenplays and training new IAS officers. In July 2020, she passed away during the Covid pandemic.

Neela's advice to women starting a new job, 'Initially the others were uncomfortable about women bosses and took me casually. Therefore: First, get to know your job well. Be it clerical or highest post, I learnt what everyone does in every department that I was posted in. Some jobs are very tough, my bosses thought I may become emotional and not be able to perform. But from the beginning I decided that I was not a woman, only an officer. When I was in the Water Transport Ministry, the job I was given was to develop 48 minor ports. I learnt the ABCD of how to develop ports and what was required from me each time I visited the upcoming port sites. I went to each and every minor site whether it was raining or sunny, on rickety barges. I researched, prepared a report that the Chief Minister took abroad to seek investments. In those two-and-a-half years as Water Transport Secretary, five jetties came up in Maharashtra, which was in itself a record.

'Second, never use excuses. I was so dedicated to my work that for many years no one in the departments came to know that I had a differently-abled son at home. My husband and daughter lent their full support and I proved my worth. Senior authorities had the confidence that I would deliver so they started giving me postings which were coveted among IAS officers – Home Secretary, I was the first Revenue Secretary, then Information and Publicity Department and Textiles Secretary.

'Women have developed that acumen to take the decisions, or show maturity. For many years my fellow officers and seniors kept taunting me that I took decisions like a woman; they meant to say that I was emotional and moved by compassion, rather than reasoning. But I ignored them because I felt compassion is a very important factor in administration. Administrators are a link between common man and the government. It is important we don't just go by a rule book alone, but act with compassion. Rules are meant for disciplining people, not to harass them. So I tried going beyond my brief and helping the people who really needed the help. They were calling that a "woman's way of looking at things" but I thought it was necessary and therefore, did not waver from my capability.'

Sally Holkar

Using woman power for sustainable community development
The lady who put Maheshwari Sarees on the World Map

Current Position: Founder of Rehwa Society, a not-for-profit foundation, working with weavers in Maheshwar, Madhya Pradesh.

A graduate of Stanford University, Sally Holkar, came to handloom when she married a member of the Indore royal family, traditional patrons of the Maheshwari saree weavers.

'At the time of my marriage, I was not at all interested in becoming a woman executive of any sort of company. So I didn't really get into the handloom aspect; it happened to me by circumstance. And unlike many other women, I didn't have to overcome many obstacles because I was the wife of someone who was a traditional figure of authority in the area. It was the weaving community of Maheshwar that approached us for help in reviving the market for Maheshwari sarees. It wasn't as if we imposed our objective on anyone and it was not a part of any particular movement, nor did we consider ourselves an NGO or have any plan. We hadn't read any books about how to do this. It was a sheer personal response, to a personal request by this community, which had been traditionally patronised by my husband's family.

'Encouraged by a wonderful person named Leela Moolgaonkar, who was the wife of the then head of Telco, Sumant Moolgaonkar. Leela herself was a very effective social welfare worker through her association with the chairman of the Tata group and her own association with the Social Welfare Board at that time. When we approached her, asking how we should take this forward, she immediately asked us to make a proposal about what we would like to do for the weaving community. We presented a proposal in an immature fashion, for we were not trained in doing so. Eventually, a grant of Rs 88,000 was given to us to train 12 women for 12 months to weave Maheshwari sarees. We were shocked to see that the grant was to train 'women' – we wanted to train men because the Maheshwar community didn't allow women to weave – they would only perform ancillary processes but not sit at the loom.

'Anyway, we had 12 looms made and cleared up some space to set them up as well as older, traditional looms from Maheshwar that hadn't been used in sixteen years. Here again, I must say that we did not have any business plans other than to help to this community. So we were very fortunate in being able to select the right women to lead this community in taking them forward. There were senior members of the

Hindu weaving community and Muslim weaving community who encouraged their women to volunteer; thereby lending authenticity to this project. We, on the other hand, were very young; I didn't even speak Hindi very well, and knew nothing about weaving. So if you are to start a **ground-level project:**

'Point 1: Be sure to start the project with communally recognised leaders in the area. By leaders, I mean people who have no political or financial motivation for working with you. We were fortunate that it happened by circumstance, and that we were not given too much money. Because quite often, when flooded with money, the project may lose its way – without knowing where it was really spent. When the money given to us had gotten over, we had many sarees in our cupboard with no idea how to sell them. So again, it was fortuitous that we found a new friend of ours – John Wilson, the founder of FabIndia, which had only one store at that time. John was American and so am I; he was into textiles and so was I, so there was an affinity there. Though FabIndia didn't sell sarees at that point of time, he asked us to display a few in a cupboard labeled 'Rewha Society,' and told us we'll see how it goes. That is how we launched Rewha Society products with independent commercial assistance given to us along with the social assistance we had from the weaving community.

'Point 2: Look around you and see who you know, directly or by extension and don't hesitate to pick up the phone and call those people and ask for their help for social welfare work because when you are doing it genuinely, there are many women who would like to come forward and help. That had us really learn what people liked or don't like. Kamala Devi Chattopadhyay offered to help organise an exhibition of these sarees in Cottage Industries. It was a great success, because all the women who came were so delighted to see the sarees they hadn't seen since their mother's and grandmother's time.

'Point 3: When you are doing a project that has to appeal to a certain market, make sure you have the right design for that market. In my case, I was trying to be Jack of all trades; I was trying to train people to weave when I didn't know weaving. I was trying to allocate budgets when I didn't know accounting and I was trying to design sarees when I hadn't worn a saree before in my life. We were fairly lucky that the weavers themselves came forward.

'I remember to this day, one of them came up and in Hindi she said, "You always put very 'English colours' in your designs, while we don't wear these colours". Naturally, I was designing what I would wear, which certainly wasn't our market. So seek outside help. It was only after 1993, that we sought designers who could design sarees. They were kind enough to accept a lesser fee than usual, because they were doing it for a charitable organisation and for the benefit of women. Where we used to have sales worth 1–1.5 lakh rupees at a 3-day exhibition, we began raking in profits of 6 lakh rupees, because the designs suited the market.

'Point 4: If you are creating a product then do so in such a way that it suits your target market; if you don't know how to design for your target audience, find somebody who does. Because that brings in financial success. Our team, committee and staff in Maheshwar, were all very financially poor weavers but they had been with us for years and we had together been designing sarees. When we decided it was time that we had templates designed for us and that we were going to pay the designer a hefty sum, they couldn't believe it. They were shocked and were against the idea of paying sombody a 100,000 rupees for doing designs that they could do themselves. But I was adamant – since we had the money, we could afford to expand. They were finally convinced when our turnover tripled; no, quadrupled in one go just because the designs were appropriate, timely and contemporary. Over time, we had progressed from 12 looms to over a 100 and without realising it, we were helping not just the women we began training to weave, but the entire Maheshwar community. We were like a design bank for them – the ones that got woven under our facility were being circulated among the entire weaving community, thereby improving their output as well. The ideas we began to generate for more efficient marketing, were also spreading through the community.

'Point 5: Hire qualified people to do whatever you need, because while you may be a charismatic leader or a good PR person, if you don't know what you are doing, at least understand what the shortcomings are and hire people who can overcome these. We understood ourselves well enough to know that we were not part of the NGO community. We didn't try to raise any more funds; instead we became self-supporting from the time that the funds we got from the social welfare grant got utilised.

'As for balancing the different roles of being a public figure yet having a personal life, I don't balance it anymore. I am in Maheshwar for 85 per cent of the time. My children are both grown up and married, and my full commitment is to this organisation. You cannot run an organisation like this from a long distance; you have to be there all the time because when you are working in rural India, it does not imply that you are working with a group of highly trained or organised people. You are working with flux and change and error so things need to be managed all the time – 24 × 7. My advice to people who think about working with people in India is that you cannot do this long distance; you have to be there. Now that we have a name for ourselves in India and globally, people who wish to collaborate with us come to Maheshwar for these projects. This is a much better way of doing things, because while they're here, they see that it is not a bogus organisation – seeing the effect we have had on the community, they become more intensely desirous of working with us. The ripple effect of that is marvelous.'

Subhashini Vasant

Picking up the strings of life after husband's passing away

Current Position: An eminent Bharatanatyam dancer, a national level artiste for the Indian Council of Cultural Relations, Doordarshan and IRCEN (India International Rural Cultural Centre). Subhashini founded Vasantharatna Foundation for Arts in memory of her husband (late) Col Vasant, Ashoka Chakra awardee.

'My husband's passing away was a huge wakeup call for me; emotionally it was my minus ground zero. I realised that there was a lot in my life I needed to be thankful for. When I married him, my life revolved around my husband. I don't regret having given the complete support. That was when I started understanding that we are a culmination of many parts.

'One part, a significant one no doubt, had gone away, but there were other parts I needed to look at. Therefore, I started breaking down my problems and started looking at them more practically. My issues such as emotional management, dealing with being a single mother, renewing my passion for dance and engaging much more intensely in it, were on my mind. Over and above all of this I had to learn financial management and had to be in control of everything. Dealing with this whole social stigma of being a widow was the toughest because in my heart I still felt like the same person…the only change was that I did not have a husband. But then the connotations society puts on the word "widow" is immense.

'My family and friends were very supportive, though there were some changes in the extended circle. I had already been exposed to a family where the *jawan* was martyred. Since Vasant was a Commander, as the lady of the unit, I had to visit the family and give them hope. When it happened to me, it made me very aware what I had to be thankful for, how much I was already blessed with, especially because those women did not have friends or family support. That's when I realised how important it is to reach out to families and friends, that's how the foundation was born.

'It started on the premise that for a single woman, the primary concern is the well-being of the children. We started with providing financial support to make sure that the children's education continue. Now we give them confidence, self-esteem; bring them to a point where they don't have to identify themselves as a widow anymore and that they are a person with their own life to lead. Just the fact that we reached out to them makes them feel they are not alone, makes a huge difference for them. Social change begins with ourselves – when we begin to look at ourselves differently, people around us look at us differently so that's when it spreads.

'I also teach dance. It helps me connect my body and mind, thaw my emotions and give it a flow. I feel, any form of exercise is essential to a child because they learn to have a passion. Any artistic outlet is a learning of life skills and is a great partner through the thick and thin of life. I feel it is very important to let a child have an artistic outlet, allowing them the space where they are not judged.

'Running the foundation is a different ball game. It has been a huge learning for me to understand how some systems work. We have to have our cause be supported. However, I will not market martyrdom, I am not going to shout that I am dealing in it but I do need funds. When people ask me what is my takeaway – I find it disgusting. First time I came home crying. Even today it is changing. Four years ago I could not even say it. Now at least I am able to say it. I am happy for the learning – it has come out of trauma, has widened my horizons.'

Shiba Maggon
Grooming talent

> *An Indian basketball player who played for the India national team. She is currently the coach for the Indian Senior women Team, as well as an international referee. She was one of the first women to qualify as a referee.*

'My dad wanted me to pursue my sister's dream. She was a basketball player, Shelly Maggon. I guess she is in a better place now. We were heartbroken when we lost her in an accident but Mom helped me to pursue my sister's dream. I guess she is in a better place; they wanted to see her as best player of the country, so fulfilled it for them. Mom wanted me to get the Indian colours. She saved money for me to buy my shoes and help me financially. She used to stitch clothes for people. I would say I did it for my sister and mother.

'I was also inspired in my game by my coach Mr Ajmer Singh and Miss Aparna Ghosh. I learnt the game by observing their game minutely.

'I used to get up 3.45 / 4 am to practice till 5.30 am. Then 5.30 to 7.30 am there was team practice. Similarly in the evening, 3.30 pm to 5pm individual skills training was there followed by team training from 5 pm to 7 pm. I did this for almost five years. I used to sleep only 5 hours daily.

'Basketball was not very popular then. But I had my own vision to develop my skills. I wanted to do something for my family. Help my mom to have a better life. I realized I had the talent to be a good athlete, but to reach top I need to put in the work extra. Even now whenever I feel I'm not able to get the best out of my players, I work with them from 5 am till 6 am, before team training starts.

'I was part of the Indian team for 7 years for different age groups. But my team did not go anywhere to play. I kept on missing different age groups. Many friends who told me it's not possible you can play India; you don't have line of travelling abroad in your hand. The more I heard it, the more I got sure about doing it.

'Even today many times people tell me things are not possible but the more I hear it more my desire gets stronger. Some relatives put restrictions, but my dad always had trust in me. I crossed all those barriers. Basically I learnt how to behave in certain circumstances. In our culture people judge you by your behavior and clothes at functions. I used to live a simple life at home and work big time away from it all. When my name started coming in newspapers, it silenced everybody. I was living in Karnal, a small city. Even today I keep it that way when I am with them, I live the Karnal life. I don't want my parents' emotions to be hurt.

'I see attitudes changing towards girls in my own city. When my cousins wanted to study, they were allowed to travel outside Karnal. I think this has helped them understand more about life.

'My students trust me more than their parents and always take my advice as to what they should do in certain situations. In the starting, students are shy about talking to each other. I guess it's the way they've been brought up. But after a week they begin to open up, begin to play their game, then things begin to get normal for them. I make it clear that they are not boys and girls but players and should act like that. When they see their coach friendly and act strong with boys and girls, they also start picking on that body language.

'Every single day when I walk on to that court and deal with players, its challenging for me. I have to make them believe that with hard work they will achieve their dreams and their goals. Every minute, every day, I have to be attuned to them. Each individual has a different mind. I have to understand their psychology and deal with them. I push them but at their own speed, not my speed as I don't want to break them.

'8 out of 10 kids get better as players. 10/10 stay in touch as I inspire them a lot about life, about athletic capability of the body. I get calls from parents thanking me for changing their ideology. They start respecting their parents, they understand the hard work their parents put in for them to see them succeed.

'I think it is important for a leader to be honest, communicate with the team. You have to be a role model for them to be inspired. Nothing demotivates me, each obstacle, each pressure of life I face I get harder, I feel I can never give up on my dreams.

'As for my detractors, the best way to treat them is through silence and resilience, prove them wrong with actions rather than words.

'I strongly believe that girls are taken as weaker gender, but they are stronger because we can bear anything. If we set the right examples, generations will follow.

'Indian women lag behind in leadership from Western women because of the way we raise kids at home. Right from the beginning when a girl is born. But life has to balance. If we make our own kids know the value of girls right from day one, treating them equal to boys, boys will know how to treat and value a girl. That's the way at later stage men will treat them women as equals.

'I want the world to know that Indian women can make their mark in basketball at international level. I coach Indian women's team, under 16 and under 18. Team has jumped to level one position 5 in Asia now. Earlier they were at level 2 position 8 or 9.

Shilpi Kapoor
Leading Innovation

> *Current Position: CEO BarrierBreak – A Digital Accessibility Firm recognized as one of the Top 15 Women Transforming India by Niti Aayog.*

'My grand dad was my role model to start with. The quality of doing things for others, taking people along, risk taking and the need to try what other people hadn't – truly a pioneer.

'To a large extent, I use his style, but also a lot of what I have seen my parents be. I think both my parents have similar natures to my granddad. Like my mom started a children's clothing store; and her sister started a nightwear business in early 1980s. That was not common for women at that time. Both had a giving nature, they were happy to do for others, not think of only self. Both were also head strong- once they made up their mind, they did it. And so do I.

'Ready to take risk, try new ideas, I guess is what I learnt from them. That's why I probably have managed to do what I do.

'I was also influenced by my ex boss. He was paralyzed and for 2 years of working with him I didn't come to know he was paralyzed. We had worked on the internet together. Using technology, he overcome challenges. He used head tracking and sip n puff technology to do a difficult job. He never looked for sympathy.

'The great thing was that I never came to know. As a security consultant/white hacker, you had to be fast. That wouldn't have been easy for him to achieve.

'As for where I want to reach, I don't have anyone that I want to be like. Just want to be me.'

'From an extended family perspective, being the second daughter was always one that I wondered about. Mostly people wondered why my parents would back me the way they did; or support me, a daughter. They supported my elder sister also but to setup an enterprise needs money. They not only supported but pumped money into my work. I see a lot of reluctance by families to invest in their daughter's business. Touch wood, she and I have had more than enough support from our parents.

'Sometimes people won't talk to you but will talk to a male member of your staff. And then when it dawns on them that you are the boss, it's an interesting reaction. I think the challenge has been more about growing a team, rather than related to me being a woman.

'Junior members are easier but when you are handling senior managers, you face challenges – attitudinal mostly!

'Personally I saw very few biases. I remember when I started off, I was 27. I would wear a saree to look older and to be taken seriously. Some people actually refer to me as the saree clad - big earring entrepreneur. Sometimes it works to your advantage – you get your first meeting; you get polite responses on the phone and more importantly people don't slam the phone on you. After that it's what you can deliver. I'm fortunate to have no such issues.

'Other than a few interviews where I didn't hire the people because of their attitude. As a woman, you know from the body language whether someone is comfortable with you, attitude that doesn't work with you. I don't like people who treat you patronizingly. So I just don't hire them. Lucky to be self-employed, I can choose who I work with.

'Interestingly the team is 50 – 50 but I do see that the

people that have stayed with me longer are women. Men leave for growth, since we aren't a company that offers a typical career growth. My ex-HR is now Head, New Initiatives at Barrierbreak. She works from home.

'We work in the social space – disability and technology. We are a social enterprise and for us profits are important but impact is equally important. This field gave me a way to do good, take people along but also do something with a difference. We are the only company of our type in this country. We brought the concept of web accessibility to India.

'I run a business where we have a lot of disabled people. We have to have emotions.

'Indian women are more flexible. We are logical as the situation demands, and flexible. We don't stick by the rules like they can't be broken; we don't see everything like black and white in the work place and I think that makes us better as leaders since we do see the human side of our teams :)

'You do want a personal life and at times this takes up more than your time and energy and so you wonder how to take it to the next level as an organization without killing yourself. I think there is more to life than only work. Women who give up work, choose what they would like to do at that point so sometimes we choose that.

'If you are employed it's about making work flexible. But as an entrepreneur, there is no such thing as flexibility. I don't see me taking this company to the next level alone but putting a team in place - so I think I have cut the umbilical cord so right now you need a person to share the workload with...and working towards growing with or without me.

'I invest my time in meeting other entrepreneurs like I did the Dasra Social Impact programme or work with TiE and organizations like Unltd India. Looking to study again soon, I hope.'

Sharn Bedi
Breaking out of a cultural context

> *Current Position: Founder at The Empower Life Company, Co-founder at Embrace Worldwide, also a TV Show Host at TV "Secrets of Womanhood", Former TV Show Host at TV "A Kitchen Abroad", Studied MBA at Monash University, Deakin University. Lives in Melbourne, Victoria, Australia.*

'My initiative is for women who are not working, to help them become more confident and happier and find their happiness and satisfaction. I feel women in India are at a better place because earlier their aspirations were at a lower level and now are at a higher level, while in the Western countries, their aspirations where at a higher plane. The difference is more in terms of Western women vs eastern women rather than Western location vs eastern location. Culturally having ethnic background means you are a woman who is divided equally between being aspirational as well as being a home maker. There is a corporate context and a cultural context.

'In the Western context, irrespective of whether you are a man or a woman, you need to be independent by the time you are 18. Whereas in our context, the moment a woman is married she goes to her husband's home. So the concept of independence is always lacking. There are multiple dynamics here at play – one is the aspiration, 2nd is the mechanisms whether they allow the aspiration to come into play, the cultural aspect and the independence .

'I will put all aspects under the independence bucket because whether it is financial freedom or physical, the attitude is one of providing protection. Sometimes the protection can be suffocating and violent or debilitating. Sometimes it hinders the aspiration. For me there are 4 anchors of woman's aspirations which remain the same whether the woman is working or not, whatever part of world she belongs to. What is different from an ethnic perspective is the concept of cultural role of a woman and the independence of a woman.

'The concept of aspiration for me is an interesting one. I grew up as the youngest and only daughter in a Punjabi family, who moved overseas as immigrants so they were not only trying to hold onto their culture from a cultural perspective which meant that they were quite strict. My dad doted on his daughter, whom he couldn't protect vs building her to become his anchor. He had two sons who were his two hands and the daughter was the doll he could dress. I had access to education but did not have the push at home to become something. As long as I got through schooling and cleared my exams I was marketable as a bride, that was the success driver for my parents.

'I had an aspiration that if I went into the university, I would become independent. Being an aggressive, assertive, stubborn, rebellious person and growing up in a Western context where you see extravagance and other women pursuing independence in college, I just wanted to prove my intelligence as equitable to the boys who were very competitive. I always used to say that anything boys can do, girls can do better. I fell in love with my university sweetheart and then proceeded to get married but for me because my in-laws were professionals – both doctors, they stressed a lot on education. They did not have a daughter so they kind of adopted me as their daughter and when I was expecting my baby, they encouraged me to pursue my education. Also because we got married at a very young age when we were still studying, it was more of a situational thing...till my husband got his feet on the ground and running.

'There was a point in time when I was the primary bread winner. Having access to those opportunities with a very open mindset, allowed me the foundation for my aspirations to flower. From a cultural perspective there was no holding back from my in-laws or my environment but yes the question came up during my maternity leave. Quite frankly, even growing up in Australia, the maternity leave component was not strong enough to help you come back to work. They were strong enough to help you have a job but not really have a career. There is a big difference between the two. So that is a challenge about women's careers – is that they may have a job but they are secondary bread winners. The income aspect vs pursuing a career. And that was something that threw me a little bit but I decided not to take it too seriously.

'And I think one of the challenges of not having a strong push at home to pursue a career, be independent, was a lack of vision on my own part about what I had potential vs reaching a goal to. So for some time the career did not necessarily progress because you pursue work as a hobby. And then after my MBA I had a baby so there is a natural desire to be at home as well as keep my resume fresh and for a long time that was the strong motivation. And then for me what was interesting was that at my age, coming in as an expat wife and then pursuing work, we got into a situation where again I needed to take a leadership role, not only as a secondary earner but as a strong one.

'What was interesting was that I got a lucky break. Where I was trying to position myself into this niche skill set which others didn't have and I had the ability to be brave – to say that yes I can do this. I had to take a risk and then teach the ropes to myself. Because, quite frankly I had never had training or mentoring or support mechanisms from a work context. But I was grateful to come across strong leaders who were willing to take a risk with me. But for some of those individuals I would not have had the lucky break or developed, specifically in the last ten years.

'For me it has not been the conventional corporate ladder. I cannot say that being overseas is the easiest path of having had career opportunities positioned in my blood stream as such, it was something that came about as a natural aspiration. And I think it is unfortunate that there are individual personalities that can make it. And that does not work for introverts or people who are not as aggressive. So that's unfortunate because it does not give every woman that opportunity to leverage that potential.

'My aspiration was more a personal vendetta against my Dad and my brothers for always believing that boys are superior. For me it came late, after my marriage and receiving encouragement from my in-laws to study further. Only in my second year I settled into my studies and saw my strengths to be a successful person. And for some reason those abilities were never appreciated or celebrated by my brothers or father or my mother, though she is very proud of me today. She was so suppressed in a nice positive way that she kind of followed the lead of my Dad. So that is where my drive came from, where I had the right support where I wanted to prove that despite being a girl I am equally capable and despite being the youngest, it was merely a matter of time where career is concerned. It is a self-driven aspiration where proving your self-worth is the driver.

'WebMD is based in New York. I started the Asia Pac office. I am employed with them. I am in the midst of creating something which is in line with this community which will eventually become a portal. Up until now I have always been employed, had lots of business ideas but always drifted away because of the need to invest heavily and make sure that kids get through schooling.

'I think in America there have been enough initiatives in Gender by the government to ensure that there is a well-balanced gender diversity. For eg you see a huge amount of women entering the work force yet you also see a huge disparity in the income of the women vs that of the man and the no. of hours they work. Quite frankly yes, US is seen in a league of its own but because the govt has pushed the initiatives. They don't have the same level of cultural norms holding them back – for eg on the financial independence parameter so they start off on an equal footing. Women who enter the workforce after educating themselves start off on a higher pay rather than the women who work and educate their way through work.

'In markets like India, Japan, China, Korea, where women don't necessarily have the same level of equality because diversity is not supported by the government b) in some of these markets, even equal access to education is missing, c) LWFP is low as post marriage women don't enter into employment or post babies because of the cost of child care. That cost plus the tax I pay; it doesn't make sense for me to work. From a perspective of Me working vs having a career and by career I don't mean being on the top but doing something of value. Where you feel like you have a role to play and a path to grow as well. I think in this context we are very far behind in the Asian markets because culturally women are not expected to have that aspiration. Culturally, they are made to feel guilty for having that aspiration and pointed out as rebels. The mechanisms are missing from the larger administration to support them.

'In Australia the situation is somewhat like the US. For eg. the last couple of months the government has put quotas with respect to diversity in senior positions. The majority of women are still in low paying jobs. We see a lot of CEOs and in politics. In Australia you are never questioned about your nationality, religion or sex. Quite frankly, there are strict discrimination laws and sexual harassment laws so women feel secure. But yet I was not in a very senior role.

'But I want to just say that I have always enjoyed being a woman, I use it to my advantage sometimes.

'I operate in my identity. And my identity is my personality, which is an outgoing, fun person. Approachable and can comfortably navigate difficult conversations. I think it is harder to work in the Indian context where hierarchies become very difficult to navigate. This became evident to me when I was working with the Indian team and they always called me Ma'am. It took me a while to get used to it and I would never call a lady Ma'am in Singapore. In a very local setting they would call their Boss Mister so and so and I was calling my boss by the first name but I quickly adapted.

'Thanks to my Western education and upbringing, I accept that I find it difficult to play along with hierarchical needs. I am appropriate for corporate Western context. Sometimes in an Indian context my personality will have to be more conservative. But once you are over 40, you can choose to be either yourself or choose to be a different person at the workplace vs who you are. Women do that. Men don't.

Men are themselves; they may be sterner at the workplace but their personality are not miles apart while women could have personalities that are miles apart.

'My style is what you get.

'That confidence is of the Western context. I have a large virtual team based around the world. They are about 30 people. In the DVD context I had a team around the world of about 120 people. Direct team is not that large. It is difficult to have bonding in a virtual context but it becomes easy when you have a personality that is expressive. It is easier to connect. Two things that you need is very strong – connection and very strong communication.

'If you are seen as genuine and humble and authentic, then they understand your intention. If you base it on human nature that everybody wants to be loved, have fun and respected and be a super star then it is easy because you are constantly doing activities that are making them all of that. I think sometime people are too task oriented and if you put too much thought into that, you end up emphasizing the why. Sometimes it is easier to just say that this is what we want to achieve in order for us to have fun. To be able to trust each other, what is it that you would like. And just listen to them. If a decision needs to be made, they respect that, if they are clear about your intention. You have to be inclusive but sometimes direct.

'My kids are in constant communication with me, I make it clear to them that I will call them back in half an hour and just calm down for now. Just pacify them. Like any other relationship, if the trust is there then you will deliver. For me it is more other way around, because for my kids I now have to stop being a Mom and coach them or mentor them. Because if my staff were to have the situation, that's what I would advise them. But when it is my kids, I act emotionally and that worsens the situation. It actually has been more a case of what can I take as learnings of my work life to make my mothering better.

'In fact when I got my lucky break, my to-be boss who was hiring asked me that you have never really worked much so how are you going to handle different clients. I just told him that I have been looking after my mother-in-law and she loves me. And I got the job. At the end of the day it is people skills and we apply them in our relationships and vice versa. Or say time management techniques for cooking.

'At the end of the day it is strength of the person and if you don't have it then you are making the same mistake in all facets of your life and that really hinders your life.

'I do a lot of research myself. I do a very wide reading myself. When it comes to development, there are a lot of areas. I am a rational person so am constantly questioning instead of accepting. So, all this goes back to principles of psychology or management written in 1800s.

If you are interested in taking a deeper look at yourself, your talents and your areas for development, then do contact us on geet.jalota@gmail.com

GEET MALA JALOTA

Geet Jalota is an author with many books to her credit and an award for one. Her experience as a Trainer and an HR professional has culminated in her writings which facilitate career growth of women. In her three-decades career solving people problems, and finding 'Right' people for jobs, she has seen what mistakes women make and this has prompted her to write books to guide them properly in their career journey. She has helped over 20K+ people improve their performances. Having interviewed innumerable candidates and worked in multiple cities, she has observed 'behaviour' in different cultural contexts and is, therefore, best poised to help people iron out their behavioural issues.

Geet is an alumnus of the Tata Institute of Social Sciences, Deonar and Commerce Department of Delhi University and member of Indian Society of Training & Development. She is friends, inspirer, motivator, guide to many youngsters who avail her services to grow in their career. She is available on aaskjobs@gmail.com

https://www.instagram.com/growcareerwithgeet/
https://www.linkedin.com/in/geetlinkedin/
Website: https://askgeet.com/